CONFLICT
IN THE GREAT
OUTDOORS

CONFLICT IN THE GREAT OUTDOORS

Toward Understanding and
Managing for Diverse Sportsmen
Preferences

Hobson Bryan

New Foreword by David Scott

The University of Alabama Press
Tuscaloosa

Typeface: Bell MT

∞

The paper on which this book is printed meets the minimum requirements
of American National Standard for Information Sciences—Permanence of
Paper for Printed Library Materials, ANSI Z39.48–1984.

Library of Congress Cataloging-in-Publication Data

Bryan, Hobson.
  Conflict in the great outdoors : toward understanding and managing for
diverse sportsmen preferences / Hobson Bryan ; new foreword by David
Scott.
      p. cm.
  Originally published: Birmingham, Ala. : Bureau of Public Administration
the University of Alabama, 1979
  Includes bibliographical references.
  ISBN 978-0-8173-5523-4 (pbk. : alk. paper) 1. Outdoor recreation--Man-
agement. 2. Outdoor recreation--Social aspects. 3. Recreation--Research. I.
Title.
  GV191.66.B79 2008
  790'.069--dc22

                                                      2008024033

CONTENTS

ILLUSTRATIONS

Figures

Tables

FOREWORD

This publication is the fourth of the Bureau of Public Administration's Sociological Studies Series. It is the product of several years of research by Professor Hobson Bryan of the Department of Sociology at The University of Alabama, in the area of outdoor recreation behavior. His objective has been to develop a conceptual framework of outdoor recreationists which would help to account for different orientations and behaviors *within* sportsmen categories. He notes that a major problem of outdoor recreation management is difficulty in identifying sportsmen subgroups having distinctive preferences and expectations as to the composition of the "quality" outdoor experience. His research points to a means of coming to grips with this conflict and diversity, and of developing management strategies accordingly.

The author provides an incisive and critical overview of social and behavioral outdoor recreation research studies. This is followed by a report of his own empirical study of trout fishermen in the Intermountain West in which he reveals the painstaking process of deriving a typology and conceptual framework to account for sportsmen diversity.

Having provided the empirical basis for the conceptual framework, the findings are linked to established sociological and psychological theories. These principles are then applied to a variety of recreation activities. In his concluding chapter, he discusses the implications of the framework for outdoor recreation theory, policy, and management.

Although The University of Alabama, as a public institution, maintains the Bureau of Public Administration for the study of public problems, nothing in this volume should be construed as a reflection of University views or policies. The author is responsible for the accuracy of his materials and for the uses and interpretations of them he has made.

JOSEPH C. PILEGGE
Acting Director
Bureau of Public Administration
The University of Alabama

FOREWORD TO THE 2008 EDITION

There are few areas of outdoor recreation or leisure research that can trace roots back to a beginning as clearly as research on recreational specialization. The specialization construct was developed by Hobson Bryan three decades ago and developed fully in his now classic, *Conflict in the Great Outdoors*. Since then, Bryan's ideas have been employed in numerous studies and applied to activities as far ranging as birdwatching, kayaking, hunting, fishing, camping, heritage tourism, and even contract bridge. The specialization construct has been primarily used as an independent variable to predict various facets of outdoor recreation participation, including sources of information used to plan trips, motivations, place attachment, sources of conflict, attitudes toward resource management, and preferences for physical and social settings. Recreational specialization continues to be a viable framework for natural resource, recreation, and event managers as they seek to develop products and services for recreation participants.

The publication of *Conflict in the Great Outdoors* in 1979 constituted a major milestone in outdoor recreation research. Prior to this, almost all studies were limited to describing the socioeconomic characteristics of outdoor recreation participants, the range of activities in which people participated, and participants' motivations and attitudes. Recognizing outdoor recreation activities included a diverse array of participants, Bryan sought to develop a framework for examining "within-sport" variability. Bryan linked theory and practice to help researchers and managers understand why groups of outdoor recreationists make demands for resources and specific policies.

Conflict in the Great Outdoors endures because Bryan put forward ideas that were intuitive and practical. One of these is that recreation participants could be arranged along a *continuum of involvement* from "casual" to "committed." Stated differently, participants in any given outdoor recreation activity vary in their level of commitment, behavior, skill and knowledge, and equipment preferences. A closely related idea is that there are characteristic styles of participation along the continuum which can be represented in the form of a *typology*. Bryan was keenly interested in identifying distinctive styles of outdoor recreation participation. His well-known typology of trout fishing is one such effort but he also developed typologies of photographers, hikers and backpackers, mountain climbers, skiers, canoeists, birdwatchers, and hunters. For Bryan, a typology was an analytic construction that would provide outdoor researchers and managers a comparative tool for examining typical behaviors and attitudes among activity participants.

Another major premise of *Conflict in the Great Outdoors* is that people have *careers* in their leisure pursuits. Bryan's typology of participation was more than just a vehicle for classifying participants along a continuum of involvement—it constituted a framework for investigating the typical stages through which people were likely to progress the longer they participated in a recreation activity. He regarded recreational specialization foremost as a *developmental process* whereby people devote themselves increasingly to a particular activity to the exclusion of others. As people progressed from one stage of involvement to another, Bryan reasoned that their motivations, setting preferences, attitudes about management practices, and attitudes toward other recreationists would change as well. He also hypothesized that progression would result in people emphasizing preservation over consumption and accentuating the quality of the recreation experience.

Finally, Bryan was among the first researchers to describe an intense style of outdoor recreation participation. Other researchers had noted that leisure could become a central life interest but little had been done to describe this status in any detail. Bryan characterized specialists as being highly skilled, knowledgeable, and committed; using advanced equipment and techniques; having distinctive orientations with regard to social and setting characteristics; and possessing a strong sense of group identification with other members of the leisure social world. First time readers of *Conflict in the Great Outdoors* will see striking similarities between Bryan's ideas about specialized participants and Robert Stebbins' concept of serious leisure (2007, *Serious leisure: A perspective for out times.* New Brunswick, N.J.: Transaction Publishers). Both ideas provide clear descriptions about people who identify strongly with their chosen pursuits and who often center their lives on these activities.

Most students of leisure today turn to Stebbins to provide guidance about people who are passionate about their leisure. Indeed, nobody has written and thought about serious leisure as has Stebbins. With this new edition of *Conflict in the Great Outdoors*, a new generation of scholars will be introduced to Hobson Bryan. They will see that Bryan also was interested in serious leisure, albeit by a different name. New readers will also see that Bryan was ahead of his time as he sought to create a framework for understanding diversity among recreation participants, and explaining how recreation participants' involvement changes. New and old readers alike will discover that *Conflict in the Great Outdoors* is as relevant today as it was when it was published originally three decades ago.

David Scott, Professor
Department of Recreation,
Park and Tourism Sciences
Texas A&M University

PREFACE

Three concerns have served as the impetus for this effort. The first relates to the continuing gap between theory and application in the social sciences. The author's contention is that "good" sociology can provide the basis for "good" management policy if the focus of research centers primarily on the *behavior* of individuals, rather than internal motivational states. This research is focused accordingly. The second concern relates to the proliferation and fragmentation of social and behavioral studies of outdoor recreation which seem not to have led to a well integrated or coherent body of knowledge. Consequently, a major part of this report is directed toward a conceptual framework of outdoor recreation behavior based on established sociological and psychological principles. And a third concern of this author, as a sportsman himself, stems from his own frustration at coping with management policies based on the supposed will of the majority or average recreationist. Consequently, in this report the attempt is to identify the numerous constituencies which comprise the average and delineate the implications of diverse sportsmen preferences for outdoor recreation management policy.

Several people made significant contributions in the conduct of this research. Special acknowledgment is due Jenny Burry Winders for her compilation and analysis of the popular literature in the "Recreation Applied" chapter of this report. Lynn Griffin is to be credited for aid with the technical literature review. Beth Ingle also assisted with the literature review and with interviews of sportsmen. Thanks are due to Brenda Hendrix, Joan Rainwater, and Betty Hughes for their clerical and typing assistance.

Appreciation is extended to John Hendee and the Pacific Northwest Forest and Range Experiment Station of the U.S. Forest Service for an initial grant (under Cooperative Agreement Number 17-PNW-75) to support development of the proposal on which this investigation is based.

The writer is especially indebted to J. B. Hilmon, Station Director, R. L. Scheer, Deputy Station Director, and Ken Cordell, Project Leader of the Southeastern Forest Experiment Station for making this project possible under the terms of Cooperative Agreement No. 18-509.

Hobson Bryan
Department of Sociology
The University of Alabama

PREFACE TO THE 2008 EDITION

Research continues on recreational specialization since publication of this work and the theory's initial formulation in the *Journal of Leisure Research* three decades or so ago. Impetus for re-publication of *Conflict in the Great Outdoors* comes not only from the ongoing stream of research around the topic, but also from the fact that, while access to the journal article remains, few still have access to the monograph. My own research shifted to other areas soon after these publications, so I now visit the arena with fresh eyes and new observations.

First, regardless of any "press toward specialization," researchers point to a mix of variables that intervenes along the way from casual participation in an activity to serious commitment. This includes affordability, marketing, opportunity, and availability of a wide array of competing activities, and such related variables as age, stage in the family life cycle, cultural values, and gender. This gauntlet of factors makes specialized or "serious leisure" problematic for a large part of the population. Then some individuals, by dent of personality, tend to dabble in a variety of life experiences, while others zealously pursue a particular activity. With leveling off or declining participation in such pursuits as hunting and fishing, advocates face a number of compelling challenges. How can participants be attracted and their participation maintained over the life cycle in the face of urban landscapes, urban values, and difficult-to-access resources? If individuals do not participate in their formative years, can they be attracted to them later and continue to be involved in these activities as adults?

Second, this monograph expands on concepts from the original journal article and deals with management issues across diverse groups and activities. If a gap remains in the current literature, it may be on the management side of the equation. Though license sales are the lifeblood of agency support, officials obviously still need to know more than how many people hunt and fish. One who participates twice a year is not the same as one who hunts every day of the season or is on the water a hundred times a year. Most mangers do not need knowledge of specialization theory to conclude that they must manage for different constituencies with different expectations, requirements, and political influence. However, specialization concepts do inform and predict what these might be and why.

Finally, management officials face more challenges than ever from a cross current of different stakeholder demands and competition for priorities over a relative static, if not declining, resource base. Human population growth and market-based forces constitute significant intervening variables in the outdoor recreation industry. Lodge and outfitting operations catering to the affluent allow individuals essentially to buy the *product* of the experience (catching fish or killing game) without the *prerequisites* of the experience—*finding* fish or game. Those who have the means are stampeding to buy properties surrounding or proximate to bountiful woods and waters and sometimes limit or deny access to publicly owned resources. Lakeside homeowners support massive applications of herbicides to control aquatic vegetation as anglers dismay over habitat loss and declining fisheries. In the meantime, the outdoor recreation industry struggles to appeal to different segments of the public, not always understanding in their marketing and merchandizing approach whether to "go Wal-Mart" or to "go Orvis." A reading of *Conflict in the Great Outdoors* will not solve these dilemmas, but it might provide a basis for fruitful discourse over a range of important issues, some that confronted us thirty years ago and some that are new on the horizon.

I am indebted to the insights and hard work of scientists and scholars in the field for modifying, correcting, and expanding my early conceptualizations of outdoor recreation and leisure behavior. Particularly valuable are articles by David Scott, Scott Shafer, and others in a 2001 issue of the *Journal of Leisure Research* critically examining the state of specialization research. I credit my fellow sociologist and friend, Jeffrey Hahn, for his early introduction of the specialization concept into the American Fisheries Society community of scientists and Robert Ditton and his students at Texas A&M for a wide range of insightful work on specialization and related topics over the years. Thanks are due to Robert Arlinghaus and Stephen Beville for sharing their own specialization bibliographies out of Germany and New Zealand respectively. The updated bibliography accompanying this monograph includes references to much of the research on specialization. However, the diverse geographic origins and interdisciplinary nature of the literature make tenuous any claim to completeness. I would be appreciative if authors whose work I missed would notify me of these omissions at hbryan@bama.ua.edu.

Hobson Bryan
March 2008

BIBLIOGRAPHY TO THE 2008 EDITION

Aas, O., W. Haider, et al. (2000). "Angler Responses to Potential Harvest Regulations in a Norwegian Sport Fishery: A Conjoint-Based Choice Modeling Approach." *North American Journal of Fisheries Management* 20(4): 940–950.

Absher, J. D. and J. R. Collins (1987). Southern Lake Michigan sportfishery: angler profiles and specialization index for Illinois and Indiana. *Illinois-Indiana Sea Grant Program Report*: 125.

Allen, M. S. and L. E. Miranda (1996). "A qualitative evaluation of specialization among crappie anglers." *American Fisheries Society Symposium* 16: 145–151.

Anderson, B. P. (1990). "Recreation specialization and preferences of Utah anglers." Masters thesis, Utah State University.

Anderson, L. E. (2003). *A comparison of activity-specific importance and management preferences among three specialization groups of trout and bass anglers.* Northeastern Recreational Research Symposium, Bolton Landing, N.Y.

Arlinghaus, R. (2006). "On the apparently striking disconnect between motivation and satisfaction in recreational fishing: the case of catch orientation of German anglers." *North American Journal of Fisheries Management* 26(3): 592–605.

Arlinghaus, R. and T. Mehner (2003). "Socio-economic characterisation of specialised common carp (Cyprinus carpio L.) anglers in Germany, and implications for inland fisheries management and eutrophication control" *Fisheries Research* 61: 19–33.

Arlinghaus, R. and T. Mehner (2005). "Determinants of management preferences of recreational anglers in Germany: Habitat management versus fish stocking." *Limnologica* 35(1–2): 2–17.

Arlinghouse, R., et al. (2007). "Understanding the complexity of catch and release in recreational fishing: An integrative synthesis of global knowledge from historical, ethical, social, and biological perspectives." *Reviews in Fishery Science*, Taylor & Francis Group, LLC. 15: 75–167.

Backlund, E. A., W. E. Hammitt, et al. (2006). "Experience use history and relationship to the importance of substitute stream attributes." *Human Dimensions of Wildlife* 11(6): 411–422.

Backman, S. J. and J. L. Crompton (1990). "Differentiating between active and passive discontinuers of two leisure activities." *Journal of Leisure Research* 22(3): 197–212.

Backman, S. J. and J. L. Crompton (1991). "Differentiating between high, spurious, latent, and low loyalty participants in two leisure activities." *Journal of Park and Recreation Administration* 9(2): 1–17.

Barker, R. M. (1989). "Tramping and Specialisation Theory: Trampers and Guided Walkers in the Greenstone Valley." Masters thesis, Lincoln University-College, Canterbury, New Zealand.

Bearden, P., M. Bennett, et al. (2006). Implications for coral reef conservation of diver specialization. *Environmental Conservation*, Foundation for Environmental Conservation Australia: 11.

Block, P. H., W. C. Black, et al. (1989). "Involvement with the equipment component of sport: Links to recreational commitment." Leisure Sciences 11: 187–200.

Brandenburg, J., W. Greiner, et al. (1982). "A conceptual model of how people adopt recreation activities." *Leisure Studies* 1: 263–276.

Brannigan, A. and A. A. McDougall (1983). "Peril and pleasure in the maintenance of a high risk sport: A study of hang-gliding." *Journal of Sport Behavior* 6: 37–51.

Brey, E. T. and X. Y. Lehto (2007). "The relationship between daily and vacation activities." *Annals of Tourism Research* 34(1): 160–180.

Bricker, E. A. and D. L. Kerstetter (2000). "Level of specialization and place attachment: An exploratory study of whitewater recreationists." *Leisure Sciences* 22(4): 233–257.

Brown, C. A. (2007). "The Carolina shaggers: Dance as serious leisure." *Journal of Leisure Research* 39(4): 623–647.

Brown, T. and W. Siemer (1991). *Toward a comprehensive understanding of angler involvement.* Northeastern Recreation Research Symposium, U. S. Forest Service.

Bryan, H. (1978). A cross-cultural comparison of leisure value systems and recreational specialization. *International Sociological Association.* Upsalla, Sweden, Sociological Abstracts.

Bryan, H. (1980). Impact of professional bass tournaments on orientation to fishing and disposition of fish. Washington, D.C., Sport Fishing Institute.

Bryan, H. (1982). A social science perspective for managing recreational conflict. *Marine Recreational Fisheries.* R. H. Stroud. Washington, D. C., Sport Fishing Institute. 7: 15–22.

Bryan, H. (2000). "Recreation specialization revisited." *Journal of Leisure Research* 32(1): 18–21.

Bryan, H. (2001). "Reply to David Scott and C. Scott Shafer, recreational specialization: A critical look at the construct." *Journal of Leisure Research* 33(3): 344–347.

Bryan, H. and N. Taylor (1987). "Toward an outdoor recreation resource policy." *Policy Studies Review* 7(2): 349–358.

Buchanan, T. (1983). "Toward an understanding of variability in satisfactions within activities." *Journal of Leisure Research*(First Quarter): 39–51.

Buchanan, T. (1985). "Commitment and leisure behavior: A theoretical perspective." *Leisure Sciences* 7: 401–420.

Burr, S. W. and D. Scott (2004). "Application of the recreational specialization framework to understanding visitors to the Great Salt Lake Bird Festival." *Event Management,* 9: 27–37.

Cessford, G. R. (1987). "Recreation in the Greenstone and Caples Valleys: For Whom and How?" *Parks, Recreation, and Tourism.* Masters Thesis, Christchurch, Canterbury, New Zealand, 212.

Chipman, B. D. and L. A. Helfrich (1988). "Recreational specialization and motivations of Virginia river anglers." *North American Journal of Fisheries Management* 8: 390–398.

Choi, S., D. K. Loomis, et al. (1994). "Effect of social group, activity, and specialization on recreation substitution decisions." *Leisure Sciences* 16(3): 143–159.

Cole, J. and D. Scott (1999). "Segmenting participation in wildlife watching: A comparison of casual wildlife watchers and serious birders." *Human Dimensions of Wildlife* 4(4): 44–61.

Colson, B. (1990). The specialization of tennis. *Sports Illustrated:* 8–12.

Crawford, D. W., E. L. Jackson, et al. (1991). "A hierarchical model of leisure constraints." *Leisure Sciences* 13: 309–320.

Curcione, N. (1980). "A reconceptualization of angler typologies." *Review of Sport & Leisure* 5: 97–113.

Dargitz, R. E. (1985). The interrelationship of occupation, job satisfraction, leisure specialization and role commitment: an exploratory study of a salmon fishing camp. *Annual Meeting of the North Central Sociological Association.* Louisville, KY: 1–45.

Dargitz, R. E. (1985). An exploratory study of a group of offshore salmon fishermen and their families on Lake Michigan. *Annual Meeting of the North Central Sociological Association.* Louisville, KY: 1–35.

Dawson, C. P. (1994). *Angler specialization among salmon and trout aanglers on Lake Ontario.* Northeastern Recreation Research Symposium, USDA Forest Service, Northeastern Forest Experiment Station, Radnor, PA.

Dawson, C. P. (1997). *Angler segmentation based on motivational scale scores.* Northeastern Recreation Research Symposium, U. S. Forest Service.

Dawson, C. P., T. L. Brown, et al. (1991). *The angler specialization concept applied: New York's Salmon River anglers.* Northwestern Recreation Research Symposium, USDA Forest Service.

Dawson, C. P., R. Ruerger, et al. (1991). *A reassessment of the angler specialization concept.* Northwestern Recreation Research Symposium, Saratoga Springs, NY.

Decker, D. J., T. L. Brown, et al. (1987). Theoretical developments in assessing social values of wildlife: Toward a comprehensive understanding of wildlife recreation involvement. *Assessing Social Values of Wildlife.* D. L. Decker and G. R. Goff. Boulder, Westview Press: 76–95.

DeVall, B. and J. Harry (1981). "Who hates whom in the great outdoors: The impacts of recreational specialization and technologies of play." *Leisure Sciences* 4: 399–418.

Ditton, R. B. (1980). *Recreational striped bass fishing: A social and economic perspective.* 5th Annual Marine Recreational Fisheries Symposium, Boston, Sport Fishing Institute.

Ditton, R. B. (1996). *Understanding the diversity among largemouth bass anglers.* American Fisheries Society Symposium.

Ditton, R. B., A. J. Fedler, et al. (1992). "The evolution of recreational fisheries management in Texas." *Ocean and Coastal Management* 17: 169–181.

Ditton, R. B., D. K. Loomis, et al. (1992). "Recreation specialization: Re-conceptualization from a social worlds perspective." *Journal of Leisure Research* 24: 33–51.

Donnelly, M. P., J. J. Vaske, et al. (1986). "Degree and range of recreation specialization: Toward a typology of boating related activities." *Journal of Leisure Research* 18: 81–95.

Donnelly, P. and K. Young (1988). "The construction and confirmation of identity in sport cultures." *Sociology of Sport Journal* 5: 223–240.

Dubin, R. (1992). *Central Life Interests: Creative Individualism in a Complex World.* New Brunswick, NJ, Transaction Publishers.

Duffus, D. A. and P. Dearden (1990). "Non-consumptive wildlife-oriented recreation: A conceptual framework." *Biological Conservation* 53: 213–231.

Ewert, A. and S. Hollenhorst (1994). "Individual and Setting Attributes of the Adventure Recreation Experience." *Leisure Sciences* 16(3): 177–191.

Falk, J. M., A. Graefe, et al. (1989). "Patterns of participation and motivation among saltwater tournament anglers." *Fisheries* 14(4): 10–17.

Fedler, A. J. and R. B. Ditton (1986). "A framework for understanding the consumptive orientation of recreational fishermen." *Environmental Management* 10(2): 221–227.

Fedler, A. J. and R. B. Ditton (1994). "Understanding angler motivations in fisheries management." *Fisheries* 19(4): 6–13.

Fedler, A. J., R. B. Ditton, et al. (1998). Factors influencing recreational fishing and boating participation. *Strategic Plan for the National Outreach and Communication Program . . . Final Report.* Washington, D. C., U. S. Fish and Wildlife Service.

Finn, K. L. and D. K. Loomis (2001). "The importance of catch motives to recreational anglers: The effects of catch satiation and deprivation." *Human Dimensions of Wildlife* 6(3): 173–187.

Fisher, M. R. (1993). "The Relationship between nonresponse bias and angler specialization." PhD diss., Texas A&M.

Fisher, M. R. (1997). "Segmentation of the angler population by catch preference, participation, and experience: A management-oriented application of recreational specialization." *North American Journal of Fisheries Management* 17: 1–10.

Floyd, M. F. and J. H. Gramann (1997). "Experience-based setting management: Implications for market segmentation of hunters." *Leisure Sciences* 19(2): 113–128.

Gahwiler, P. and M. E. Havitz (1998). "Toward a relational understanding of leisure social worlds, involvement, psychological commitment, and behavioral loyalty." *Leisure Sciences* 20(1): 1–23.

Gigliotti, L. M. and R. B. Payton (1993). "Values and behaviors of trout anglers, and their attitudes toward fishery management relative to membership in fishing organizations: A Michigan case study." *North American Journal of Fisheries Management* 13: 492–501.

Gill, A. R. (1980). The social circle of catfishermen: a contribution to the sociology of fishing. PhD diss., Kansas State University.

Graefe, A. (1980). The relationship between level of participation and selected aspects of specialization in recreational fishing. PhD diss., Texas A&M.

Graefe, A. (1981). Understanding diverse fishing groups: The case of drum fishermen. *Marine Recreational Fisheries*. H. Clepper. Washington, C. C., Sports Fishing Institute. 6: 69–79.

Graefe, A., M. P. Donnelly, et al. (1986). *Crowding and specialization: A reexamination of the crowding model.* National Wilderness Research Conference, U. S. Forest Service.

Griffin, J. (1985). Recreation specialization and satisfactions of Alabama hunters. Masters thesis, University of Alabama.

Hahn, J. (1991). Angler specialisation: measurement of a key sociological concept and implications for fisheries management decisions. In: Guthrie, D., Hoenig, J.M., et al. (Eds.), Creel and Angler Surveys in Fisheries Management, Proceedings of the American Fisheries Society Symposium, vol. 12, Bethesda, MD, pp. 380–389.

Hailu, G., P. C. Boxall, et al. (2005). "The influence of place attachment on recreation demand." *Journal of Economic Psychology* 26(4): 581–598.

Hammitt, W. E., E. A. Backlund, et al. (2004). "Experience use history, place bonding and resource substitution of trout anglers during recreation engagements." *Journal of Leisure Research* 36(3): 356–378.

Hammitt, W. E., L. Knauf, et al. (1989). "A comparison of user versus researcher determined level of past experience on recreation preference." *Journal of Leisure Research* 21: 202–213.

Hammitt, W. E. and C. D. McDonald (1983). "Past on-site experience and its relationship to managing river recreation resources." *Forest Science* 29: 262–266.

Hammitt, W. E., C. D. McDonald, et al. (1986). *Experience level and participation motives of winter wilderness users.* National Wilderness Research Conference, USDA Forest Service.

Harrington, M., G. Cuskelly, et al. (2000). "Career volunteering in commodity-intensive serious leisure: Motorsport events and their dependence on volunteers/amateurs." *Loisir & Societe-Society and Leisure* 23(2): 421–452.

Hase, H. J. (1996). The effects of angling specialization on the motivations and management setting preferences of Arizona warmwater anglers. Masters thesis, Arizona State University.

Hase, H. J., R. J. Virden, et al. (1996). *Motivation, perceived conflict, and management preference variations among low, medium, and high angling specialists.* Leisure Research Symposium, Kansas City.

Havengaard, G. T. (2002). "Birder specialization differences in conservation involvement, demographics, and motivations." *Human Dimensions of Wildlife* 7(1): 21–36.

Havitz, M. E. and F. Dimanche (1997). "Leisure involvement revisited: Conceptual conundrums and measurement advances." *Journal of Leisure Research* 29(3): 245–278.

Havitz, M. E. and F. Dimanche (1999). "Leisure involvement revisited: Drive properties and paradoxes." *Journal of Leisure Research* 31(2): 122–149.

Henderson, K. A. (2000). "False dichotomies, intellectual diversity, and the "either/or" world: Leisure research in transition." *Journal of Leisure Research* 32: 49–53.

Hollenhorst, S. (1990). What makes a recreation specialist? The case of rock-climbing. *Social Science and Natural Resource Recreation Management.* Boulder, Westview Press: 81–90.

Hollenhorst, S. J. (1988). The relationship between recreation specialization and characteristics, behaviors and preferences of selected rock climbers [microform]. *College of Human Development and Performance.* PhD diss., Ohio State University.

Hopkins, T. and R. Moore (1994). *The relationship of recreation specialization to the setting preferences of mountain bicyclists.* Northwestern Recreation Research Symposium, Radnor, Pennsylvania, USDA Forest Service.

Hunt, L. M. (2005). "Recreational Fishing Site Choice Models: Insights and Future Opportunities." *Human Dimensions of Wildlife* 10(3): 153–172.

Hunt, L. M., W. Haider, et al. (2005). "Accounting for varying setting preferences among moose hunters." *Leisure Sciences* 27(4): 297–314.

Hutt, C. P. and P. W. Bettoli (2007). "Preferences, specialization, and management attitudes of trout anglers fishing in Tennessee tailwaters." *North American Journal of Fisheries Management* 27(4): 1257–1267.

Hvenegaard, G. T. (2002). "Birder Specialization Differences in Conservation Involvement, Demographics, and Motivations." *Human Dimensions of Wildlife* 7(1): 21–36.

Hwang, S. N., C. Lee, et al. (2005). "The relationship among tourists' involvement, place attachment and interpretation satisfaction in Taiwan's national parks." *Tourism Management* 26(2): 143–156.

Jacob, G. R. (1980). "Conflict in outdoor recreation." *Journal of Leisure Research*(Fourth Quarter): 369–380.

Katz, M. S. (1978). An Assessment of the Conservation Attitudes of Sport Fishing Participants, Pennsylvania State University, College of Health, Physical Education and Recreation: 196.

Kaufman, R. B. (1982). The relationship between activity specialization and resource related attitudes and expected rewards of canoeists. PhD diss., University of Maryland.

Kerins, A. (2005). Relax dude, we just play for fun! The flatlining trajectory of recreation specialization in the context of ultimate frisbee. College Station, Texas A@M University.

Kim, S. S., D. Scott, et al. (1997). "An exploration of the relationships among social psychological involvement, behavioral involvement, commitment, and future intentions in the context of birdwatching." *Journal of Leisure Research* 29(3): 320–341.

Knopf, R. C., G. L. Peterson, et al. (1983). "Motives for recreational river floating: Relative consistency across settings." *Leisure Sciences* 5(3): 231–255.

Kuentzel, W. F. (2001). "How specialized is specialization research?" *Journal of Leisure Research* 33(3): 351–365.

Kuentzel, W. F. and T. A. Heberlein (1992). "Does specialization affect behavioral choices and quality judgments among hunters." *Leisure Sciences* 14: 211–226.

Kuentzel, W. F. and T. A. Heberlein (1997). "Social status, self-development, and the process of sailing specialization." *Journal of Leisure Research* 29: 300–319.

Kuentzel, W. F. and T. A. Heberlein (2006). "From novice to expert? A panel study of specialization progression and change." *Journal of Leisure Research* 38(4): 496–512.

Kuentzel, W. F. and C. D. McDonald (1992). "Differential effects of past experience, commitment and lifestyle dimensions on river use specialization." *Journal of Leisure Research* 24: 269–287.

Kyle, G., E. A. Bricker, et al. (2004). "An examination of recreationists' relationships with activities and settings." *Leisure Sciences* 26(2): 123–142.

Kyle, G., A. Graefe, et al. (2003). "An examination of the relationship between leisure activity involvement and place attachment among hikers along the Appalachian Trail." *Journal of Leisure Research* 35(3): 249–273.

Kyle, G., W. Norman, et al. (2007). "Segmenting anglers using their consumptive orientation profiles." *Human Dimensions of Wildlife* 12(2): 115–132.

Lee, J. H. and D. Scott (2004). "Measuring birding specialization: A confirmatory factor analysis." *Leisure Sciences* 26(3): 245–260.

Lee, J. H. and D. Scott (2006). "For better or worse? A structural model of the benefits and costs associated with recreational specialization." *Leisure Sciences* 28(1): 17–22.

Lee, S. H., A. R. graefe, et al. (2007). "The effects of specialization and gender on motivations and preferences for site attributes in paddling." *Leisure Sciences* 29(4): 355–373.

Lemelin, R. H., et al. (2008). "Polar bear viewers as deep ecotourists: How specialised are they?" *Journal of Sustainable Tourism* 16(1).

Little, B. R. (1976). Specialization and the varieties of environmental experience: Empirical studies within the personality paradigm. *Experiencing the Environment.* S. Wapner, S. B. Cohen, and B. Kaplan. New York, Plenium Press: 81–116.

Liu, S. (2008). Level of specialization and place attachment of anglers. *Institute of Tourism and Recreation Management,* Masters Thesis, NSYSU, 106.

Lloyd, G. S. (1993). An examination of the relationship between angler specialization and constraints to trout fishing. *College of Health and Human Development.* Master thesis, State College, Pennsylvania State University, 99.

Loomis, D. K., L. E. Anderson, et al. (2004). *Recreation specialization and fishing mode: Effects on activity and nonactivity-specific Motivations.* 16th Annual NERR Symposium.

Loomis, D. K. and R. B. Ditton (1987). "Analysis of motive and participation differences between saltwater sport and tournament fishermen." *North American Journal of Fisheries Management* 7: 482–487.

Loomis, D. K. and S. Holland (1997). *Specialization and sport fishing: Angler support for rules and regulations.* Gulf and Caribbean Fisheries Institute.

Loomis, D. K. and M. Ross (2000). *A comparison of trout and bass anglers on catch-related measures according to specialization level.* 130th Annual Meeting of the American Fisheries Society, St. Louis, MO.

Loomis, D. K. and R. A. Salz (2001). *An investigation of Massachusetts saltwater angler motives and attitudes across recreation specialization and fishing mode.* Northeast Recreation Research Symposium, Bolton Landing, N. Y.

Loomis, D. K. and R. B. Warnick (1991). *Recreational specialization and the analysis of angler differences according to age cohort.* Northeast Recreation Research Symposium, U. S. Forest Service.

MacKay, K. J. and J. L. Crompton (1998). "Alternative typologies for leisure programs." *Journal of Park and Recreation Administration* 6(4): 53–65.

Mackellar (2006). "Fanatics, fans or just good fun: Travel behaviours and motivations of the fanatic." *Journal of Vacation Marketing* 12(3): 195–217.

Manfredo, M. J. (1989). "An investigation of the basis for external information search in recreation and tourism." *Leisure Sciences* 11: 29–45.

Manfredo, M. J. and B. P. Anderson (1982). Recreation preferences of Oregon trout fishermen. *Miscellaneous Report 18.* St. Paul: 64–68.

Manning, R. E. (1999). Specialization in recreation: Experience and related concepts. *Studies in Outdoor Recreation: Search and Research for Satisfaction, 2nd ed.* R. E. Manning. Corvallis, Oregon State University Press: 222–237.

Margenau, T. L. and J. P. Petchenik (2004). "Social aspects of muskellunge management in Wisconsin." *North American Journal of Fisheries Management* 24: 82–94.

Martin, S. R. (1997). "Specialization and differences in setting preferences among wildlife viewers." *Human Dimensions of Wildlife* 2(1): 1–18.

McFarlane, B. L. (1994). "Specialization and motivations of birdwatchers." *Wildlife Society Bulletin* 22(3): 361–370.

McFarlane, B. L. (1996). "Socialization influences of specialization among birdwatchers." *Human Dimensions of Wildlife* 1(1): 35–50.

McFarlane, B. L. (2001). "Comments on Recreational Specialization: A Critical Look at the Construct." *Journal of Leisure Research* 33(3): 348–351.

McFarlane, B. L. (2004). "Recreation specialization and site choice among vehicle-based campers." *Leisure Sciences* 26(3): 309–322.

McFarlane, B. L. and P. Boxall (1996). "Participation in wildlife conservation by birdwatchers." *Human Dimensions of Wildlife* 1(3): 1–14.

McFarlane, B. L., P. C. Boxwell, et al. (1996). "Exploring forest and recreation management preferences of forest recreationists in Alberta." *Forestry Chronicle* 72(6): 623–629.

McFarlane, B. L., P. C. Boxall, et al. (1998). "Past experience and behavioral choice among wilderness users." *Journal of Leisure Research* 30(2): 195–213.

McGurrin, J. M. (1986). *Diversity in Gunpowder River trout anglers and implications for management.* Annual Conference of Southeastern Association Fish and Wildlife Agencies.

McIntyre, N. (1989). "The personal meaning of participation : Enduring involvement." *Journal of Leisure Research* 21: 167–179.

McIntyre, N. and J. J. Pigram (1992). "Recreation specialization reexamined: The case of vehicle-based campers." *Leisure Sciences* 14(1): 3–15.

Merrill, K. and A. Graefe (1998). *The relationship between activity specialization and preferences for setting and route attributes of selected rock climbers.* Northeastern Recreation Research Symposium, U. S. Forest Service.

Meyer, L. A. (2002). Recreation specialization and environmental behaviors: An exploratory analysis among scuba divers. *Recreation, Parks, and Tourism,* Masters thesis, University of Florida.

Miller, C. A. (1997). Recreation specialization and attitudes toward wildlife management polices among Pennsylvania hunter. PhD diss., Pennsylvania State.

Miller, C. A. and A. R. Graefe (2000). "Degree and range of specialization across related hunting activities." *Leisure Sciences* 22(3): 195–204.

Moldovanyi, A., C. Pierskalla, et al. (2002). *Examining specialization for a fishing subactivity: Is activity and place specialization better understood at the activity or subactivity level?.* Proceedings of the 2004 Northeastern Recreation Research Symposium.

Morgan, M. (2006). "The social hierarchy of fishing: myth or reality?" *Human Dimensions of Wildlife* 11(5): 317–327.

Morgan, M. and J. Soucy (2006). "Usage and evaluation of nonformal environmental education services at a state park: Are anglers catching more than fish?" *Environmental Education Research* 12(5): 595–608.

Mowen, A., D. R. Williams, et al. (1996). *Specialized participants and their environmental attitudes: Re-examining the role of "traditional" and psychological specialization dimensions.* Northeastern Recreation Research Symposium, U. S. Forest Service.

Needham, M. C., J. J. Vaske, et al. (2007). "Hunting specialization and its relationship to participation in response to chronic wasting disease." *Journal of Leisure Research* 39(3): 413–437.

Ninomiya, H. and H. Kikuchi (2004). "Recreation specialization and participant preferences among windsurfers." *International Journal of Sport and Health Science* 2: 1–7.

O'Leary, J. T. (1985). Impact of recreation activity specialization on management and program support for water resources. West Lafayette, IN, Purdue University: 49.

Oh, C. O. (2005). Understanding recreationists' attitudes toward and preferences for natural resources conservation, PhD diss., Texas A&M.

Oh, C. O. and R. B. Ditton (2006). "Using recreation specialization to understand multi-attribute management preferences." *Leisure Sciences* 28(4): 369–384.

Oh, C. O., R. B. Ditton, et al. (2005). "Understanding differences in nonmarket valuation by angler specialization level." *Leisure Sciences* 27(3): 263–277.

Quinn, S. P. (1992). "Angler perspectives on walleye management." *North American Journal of Fisheries Management* 12: 367–378.

Quinn, S. P. (1996). "Trends in regulatory and voluntary catch-and-release fishing." *American Fisheries Society Symposium* 16: 152–162.

Ramthun, R. (1995). "Factors in user group conflict between hikers and mountain bikers." *Leisure Sciences* 17: 159–169.

Reid, I. S. and J. L. Crompton (1993). "A taxonomy of leisure purchase decision paradigms based on level of involvement." *Journal of Leisure Research* 25(2): 182–202.

Riechers, R., G. R. Wilde, et al. (1991). *Freshwater and saltwater anglers: A comparative analysis of differences in attitudes toward management tools.* Annual Conference of Southeastern Association of Fish and Wildlife Agencies.

Romberg, W. J. (1999). Market segmentation, preferences, and management attitudes of Alaska nonresident anglers. *Fisheries and Wildlife Sciences.* Masters thesis, Virginia Polytechnic Institute and State University.

Rouphael, A. B. and G. J. Inglis (2001). "Take only photographs and leave only footprints"?: An experimental study of the impacts of underwater photographers on coral reef dive sites." *Biological Conservation* 100(3): 281–287.

Salz, R. A. and D. K. Loomis (1999). *A specialization index for angler segmentation: Index effectiveness and comparisons between modes.* Northeastern Recreation Research Symposium, Bolton Landing, N. Y.

Salz, R. A. and D. K. Loomis (2001). *Constraints and recreation specialization among Massachusetts saltwater anglers.* Northeast Recreation Research Symposium, Bolton Landing, N. Y.

Salz, R. A. and D. K. Loomis (2002). *Testing the role of recreation specialization as a moderating variables within the cognitive hierarchy model.* Northeast Recreational Research Symposium.

Salz, R. A., D. K. Loomis, et al. (2004). *Effect of recreation specialization on angler avidity across different fishing modes and water types.* Northeastern Research Symposium, Bolton Landing, N. Y.

Salz, R. J. and D. K. Loomis (2005). "Recreation specialization and anglers' attitudes towards restricted fishing areas." *Human Dimensions of Wildlife* 10: 187–199.

Salz, R. J., D. K. Loomis, et al. (2001). A Baseline Socio-economic Study of Massachusetts' Marine Recreational Fisheries. *NOAA Technical Memorandum NMFS NE* 165.

Salz, R. J., D. K. Loomis, et al. (2001). "Development and validation of a specialization index and testing of specialization theory." *Human Dimensions of Wildlife* 6(4): 239–258.

Salz, R. J. and C. S. Shafer (2001). "Recreational specialization: A critical look at the construct." *Journal of Leisure Research* 33(3): 319–343.

Sanyal, N. and W. J. McLaughlin (1990). Identifying different types of Idaho anglers: A pilot analysis using 1988 Idaho angler opinion survey data.

Sanyal, N. and W. J. McLaughlin (1993). Angler market segmentation, angler satisfaction, and activity persistence among Idahoans. Moscow, Idaho, University of Idaho Department of Resource Recreation and Tourism. 1992 Annual Report to Idaho Fish and Game.

Schoolmaster, F. A. and J. W. Frazier (1985). "An analysis of angler preferences for fishery management strategies." *Leisure Sciences* 7(3): 321–343.

Schramm, H. L. and P. D. Gerard (2004). "Temporal changes in fishing motivation among fishing club anglers in the United States." *Fisheries Management and Ecology* 11(5): 313–321.

Schreyer, R. (1982). Experience level affects expectations for recreation participation. *Forest and River Recreation: Research Update.* St. Paul: 154–159.

Schreyer, R. and J. T. Beaulieu (1986). "Attribute preference for wildland recreation settings." *Journal of Leisure Research* 18(4): 231–247.

Schreyer, R. and R. C. Knopf (1990). "The effect of experience use history on the multidimensional structure of motivations to participate in leisure activities." *Journal of Leisure Research* 22: 36–54.

Schreyer, R., D. W. Lime, et al. (1984). "Characterizing the influence of past experience on recreation behavior." *Journal of Leisure Research*(First Quarter): 35–51.

Schreyer, R. and D. W. Lime (1984). "A novice isn't necessarily a novice: The influence of experience use history on subjective perceptions of recreation participation." *Leisure Sciences* 6(2): 131–149.

Scott, D., R. B. Ditton, et al. (2005). "Measuring specialization among birders: Utility of a self-classification measure." *Human Dimensions of Wildlife* 10(1): 53–75.

Scott, D. and G. Godbey (1992). "An analysis of adult play groups: Social versus serious participation in contract bridge." *Leisure Sciences* 14: 47–67.

Scott, D. and G. Godbey (1994). "Recreation specialization in the social world of contract bridge." *Journal of Leisure Research* 26: 275–295.

Scott, D. and C. S. Shafer (2001). "Recreational specialization: A critical look at the construct." *Journal of Leisure Research* 33(3): 319–343.

Selin, S. W. and D. R. Howard (1988). "Ego involvement and leisure behavior: A conceptual specification." *Journal of Leisure Research* 20(3): 237–244.

Shafer, C. S. and W. E. Hammitt (1995). "Purism revisited: Specifying recreational conditions of concern according to resource intent" *Leisure Sciences* 17(1): 15–30.

Smith, C. L. and R. McKelvey (1986). "Specialist and generalist: Roles for coping with variability." *North American Journal of Fisheries Management* 6(1): 88–99.

Stebbins, R. A. (1992). *Amateurs, Professionals, and Serious Leisure.* Montreal, McGill-Queen University Press.

Steele, R. J., S. Burr, et al. (1990). *Pennsylvania trout fishing: a consideration of specialization and social interaction.* Northeastern Recreation Research Symposium, USDA Forest Service.

Strauss, A. (1984). "Social worlds and their segmentation processes." *Studies in Symbolic Interaction* 5: 123–139.

Sutton, S. G. (2001). "Understanding catch-and-release behavior of recreational anglers." *Parks and Recreation.* PhD diss., Texas A&M.

Tarrant, M., H. Cordell, et al. (1997). "Measuring perceived crowding for high density river recreation." *Leisure Sciences* 19: 97–112.

Tarrant, M., M. J. Manfredo, et al. (1994). "Recollections of outdoor recreation experiences: A psychophysiological perspective." *Journal of Leisure Research* 26: 357–371.

Thapa, B., A. R. Graefe, et al. (2005). "Moderator and mediator effects of scuba diving specialization on marine-based environmental knowledge-behavior contingency." *Journal of Environmental Education* 37(1): 53–68.

Thapa, B., A. R. Graefe, et al. (2006). "Specialization and marine based environmental behaviors among SCUBA divers." *Journal of Leisure Research* 38(4): 601–615.

Trauer, B. (2006). "Conceptualizing special interest tourism: Frameworks for analysis." *Tourism Management* 27(2): 183–200.

Valentine, B. (2003). Recreation specialization: Upper Manistee River shoreline owner anglers and their management preferences. *Northeastern Recreation Research Symposium.* Bolton Landing, NY.

Van Liere, K. D. and F. P. Noe (1981). "Outdoor recreation and environmental attitudes: Further examination of the Dunlap-Heffernan thesis." *Rural Sociology* 46(3): 505–515.

Vaske, J., R. Dyar, et al. (2004). "Skill level and recreation conflict among skiers and snowboarders." *Leisure Sciences* 26: 215–225.

Virden, R. J. (1991). "Integrating past experience into leisure marketing strategies." *Leisure Information Quarterly* 16(3): 6–8.

Virden, R. J. and R. Schreyer (1988). "Recreation specialization as an indicator of environmental preference." *Environment and Behavior* 20: 721–739.

Vitters, J. (1997). "Cognitive schemes and affective experience: The case of angler specialization." *Human Dimensions of Wildlife* 2(4): 10–21.

Warner, W. S. (1982). Image specialization: A study of stereotypes for cross-country skiers and trout fishermen in Main, University of Main. Masters.

Watson, A. E. and J. J. Niccolucci (1992). "Defining past-experience dimensions for wilderness recreation." *Leisure Sciences* 14: 89–103.

Watson, A. E. and J. J. Niccolucci (1994). "The nature of conflict between hikers and recreational stock users in the Jonn Muir Wilderness." *Journal of Leisure Research* 26(4): 372–378.

Watson, A. E., J. W. Roggenbuck, et al. (1991). "The influence of past experience on wilderness choice." *Journal of Leisure Research* 23: 21–36.

Wellman, J. D., J. W. Roggenbuck, et al. (1982). "Recreation specialization and norms of depreciative behavior among canoeists." *Journal of Leisure Research* 14: 323–340.

Wilde, G. R. and R. B. Ditton (1994). "A management-oriented approach to understanding diversity among largemouth bass anglers." *North American Journal of Fisheries Management* 14: 34–40.

Wilde, G. R. and R. K. Riechers (1992). *Demographic and social characteristics and management preferences of Texas freshwater catfish anglers.* Forty-Sixth Annual Conference Southeastern Association of Fish and Wildlife Agencies, Corpus Christie.

Wilde, G. R., R. K. Robinson, et al. (1998). "Differences in attitudes, fishing motives, and demographic characteristics between tournament and nontournament black bass anglers in Texas." *North American Journal of Fisheries Management* 18: 422–431.

Williams, D. R. (1985). *A developmental model of recreation choice behavior.* Symposium on Recreation Choice Behavior, U. S. Forest Service.

Williams, D. R. and M. G. Huffman (1985). *Recreation specialization as a factor in backcountry trail choice.* National Wilderness Research Conference, Fort Collins.

Williams, D. R., M. Patterson, et al. (1992). "Beyond the commodity metaphor: Examining emotional and symbolic attachment to place." *Leisure Sciences* 14: 29–46.

Wright, M. V. and N. Sanyal (1998). "Differentiating motivations of guided versus unguided fly anglers." *Human Dimensions of Wildlife* 3(1): 34–46.

Yoder, D. G. (1997). "A model for commodity intensive serious leisure." *Journal of Leisure Research* 29(4): 407–429.

Young, G. (1998). *Recreation specialization and attitudes toward wetland protection.*

Young, J., D. R. Williams, et al. (1990). *The role of involvement in identifying users' preferences for social standards in the Cohutta Wilderness.* Southeastern Recreation Research Conference, U. S. Forest Service.

CONFLICT
IN THE GREAT
OUTDOORS

CHAPTER I

Introduction

The object of this report is to provide a conceptual framework for a typology of outdoor recreationists. Developing sociological information about natural resource users has become critically important for resource management. Land-use planners and managers need to know about the preferences and behavior of their clients, on whom they are ultimately dependent for support. Knowing the kinds of experiences sought by users is fundamental to providing them and minimizing conflicts among different groups of users.

In fact, as population pressures mount and the popularity of outdoor recreation increases, conflicts among recreationists may become the primary problem of outdoor management. In short, the problem is to allocate scarce resources sought by recreationists with different expectancies and requirements. Even now agency heads are buffeted from all sides by competing groups. Reservoir fishermen want restrictions on water-skiers; backpackers ask for a ban on things "artificial," from roads and motorized vehicles to developed trails and horses. Some trout fishermen plead for more waters with catch-and-release policies while others want raised bag limits and more stocking. Campers want more developed campgrounds; others want more primitive areas.

In the meantime, outdoor equipment manufacturers promote the fun of using their contrivances in the great outdoors, and more and more people listen and buy. Snowmobilers may actually have violent confrontations with cross-country skiers as the latter argue that the wilderness solitude they seek is being denied to them. While trail bikes roar into the backcountry offending the wilderness hiker, bass boats hydroplane across reservoirs making canoeists and small boaters fear for their lives. Swimming anyone?

Then there is the issue of consumptive versus nonconsumptive uses of wildlife. Is the birdwatcher to be given preference over the hunter? And what is it that hunters really want anyway? Anti-hunting forces argue that the essence of the sport is in the "murder" of the animal. Spokesmen for the hunters point to the research that indicates that it is the pursuit and challenge of the game, even the social aspects of the hunt, that appeal to the hunter, not the actual kill. Yet there are hunters who complain of low bag limits and limited opportunities for a kill.

As if there were not enough confusion, resource managers must rely on an uncoordinated jumble of social and human behavioral studies of outdoor recreationists. The findings may be so abstract that they seem to have little practical application, or they may proceed from different (and often unstated) premises. Managers complain that the studies are too detailed, ("Spring Stream Flyfishermen of Madison County"), too esoteric ("Tension Release Among Quail Hunters") – too general ("Hunting and Fishing in the United States"), or too manifest ("Why People Eat Fish").

All of this points to a critical need, then, for more information on which managers can base their decisions, but information that has been synthesized and organized in a fashion that lends itself to easy interpretation and application. The major premise underlying the effort reported here is that a typology based on a conceptual framework of outdoor recreationists will (1) serve to lend direction and organization to existing studies and (2) enable managers to apply much more effectively already established social and behavioral principles to everyday management problems.

As a matter of fact, sociological information about diverse groups of people (or any other kind of information, for that matter) is generalized using typologies based on some kind of conceptual framework. Informally, of course, almost everyone categorizes or types things and people they encounter based on their personal information. Consider the number of times someone refers to "this kind and that kind of person," or "this kind and that kind of fisherman." When making such references, people are using their own typologies based on their personal experience and other sources of information (much of it selectively perceived). However, scientific compilation of sociological information can also be used to develop typologies that are based on reliable and valid data and guided by frameworks grounded in existing scientific study and practical experience.

Recognition of sportsmen heterogeneity and the management implications comes from a number of quarters. Hendee's (1974) "multiple-satisfaction approach to game management" is an example of the importance of the concept in hunting (though one of the illustrations in his article comes from steelhead fishing). Building on his and his colleagues' work (Hendee, et al., 1968; Clark, et al., 1971), he concludes:

> Different kinds of experiences are sought by participants in the same activity, be it wilderness hiking, car camping or fishing. One may have several reasons for seeking outdoor recreation, and all or some of those reasons may differ from those which attract other participants to the same activity. (Hendee, 1974:106)

Another key implication of the need to correctly identify and categorize recreationists is that what is a "quality" outdoor experience to one sportsman is not to another (Talhelm, 1973). Although the notion of quality is relative, a value judgment, the concept can be operationalized for management decision purposes. Hendee offers the cogent definition of quality as "the relationship between satisfactions anticipated in an outdoor experience and satisfactions realized" (Hendee, 1974). In other words, quality depends on what the individual is looking for and how much of it he gets. A crucial problem for resource managers, then, is to determine what different sportsmen are seeking, and how it can be delivered within existing constraints. The problem is matching recreationists' desires for different kinds of experience with appropriate resources managed to produce those experiences.

Harry, Hendee, and Stein's (1972) "resource specificity" concept is consistent with recognition of increasing needs and demands of the more specialized sportsman. They suggest that since motivations of outdoor recreationists can be ordered on a continuum from the most general to the most specific "user welfare would be optimized by resolving conflicts in favor of users attracted by the most specific motives" (Harry, et al., 1972:4). Their rationale is that users with more "general" motivations and requirements for their satisfaction have alternative activities and situations by which they can satisfy their recreation desires. Persons with specific preferences and requirements are completely disfranchised if opportunities for their desires are not met, whereas "generally" motivated users have more numerous alternatives. This notion is politically viable as well, for the specialized users are often the most organized and vocal. And no wonder — they consider themselves as having the most at stake in terms of personal commitment and involvement in their sport.

Thus, by one sociological criterion at least, managers may be faced with the problem of matching resources with more users having increasingly specific motivations. But such optimum resource utilization — and any other allocation or management strategy — depends upon an accurate classification of sportsmen by user type. The need is to derive a conceptually and empirically sound basis for identifying various categories of recreationists and the orientations which shape their resource desires and requirements.

Study Strategy

Development of a conceptual framework and typology of recreationists relevant to resource management decisions and strategies is different from a simple ad hoc classificatory system where more or less arbitrary classes are constructed to summarize data and form descriptive taxonomies. Classification schemes and taxonomies are descriptive rather than analytical — their categories are not linked together in ways that can lead to explanatory predictive theories.[1]

---

[1] In classificatory systems "no attempt is made to fit classes to data so that relations between variables and dimensions can be summarized; the classes are independent of one another" (Denzin, 1970:66). The categorical system, or taxonomy, on the other hand, ideally bears a close relationship to empirical

This proposed effort goes further in that the object of a conceptual framework (and its accompanying typology) is for descriptive categories to be ". . . placed within a broad structure of both explicit and assumed propositions" (Denzin, 1970:67). The primary advantage of this scheme over simple classificatory systems and taxonomies is that propositions are summarized and explanations proposed for large amounts of data.

Conceptual frameworks logically direct empirical and theoretical activity around a core set of problems and, as such, offer the beginnings of systematic theory. Thus, this effort builds on the findings of this researcher and others in an attempt to develop explanatory principles of recreational behavior. Among the lines of inquiry followed are desired outdoor recreation experiences, social grouping during participation, specialization in equipment, type of behavior, and degree of leisure commitment.

Procedures

The study encompasses the following stages:

1. A wide-ranging literature review was undertaken to provide information about the content and nature of various recreational activities.

2. Interviews were conducted with highly skilled and knowledgeable individuals in different sports to supplement and validate inferences drawn from the literature.

3. The literature review required access to major holdings in the outdoor recreation area, therefore the Denver Conservation Library was visited and interlibrary loan services were utilized to supplement University of Alabama resources.

---

reality and consists of a system of classes so that the relationships among them can be described. In other words, categories are formed to fit the data and there are interrelationships between categories. Though taxonomies perform several functions — specify units of reality to be analyzed, indicate how units may be described (Zetterberg, 1965:24-28), generally guide the investigation and tell the researcher what to look for — they remain in the descriptive rather than the analytical realm and are not as powerful as the conceptual framework. Taxonomies are merely first step efforts in anticipation of research leading to explanatory and predictive theories.

4. Consultation was undertaken with authorities in the U.S. Forest Service and spokesmen familiar with respective areas of outdoor recreation activity in the United States and Canada. Consultation was also conducted with less accessible individuals through correspondence and telephone conversations.

The product of this effort is a report which encompasses a broad look at the nature and variety of outdoor recreation activity and organizes this activity in terms of social and behavioral principles. The hope is that the framework will be of value both as a rationale and as a tool for authorities as they attempt to resolve user conflicts over resource allocation and management.

Verificational studies are recommended as a second stage of this effort. But this initial investigation attempts to determine who the various recreationists are, what they are seeking, and by what principles they are guided. The section to follow is a critique of the existing outdoor recreation research which sets the stage for the approach detailed in the subsequent sections of the report.

REFERENCES

Clark, R. N., J. C. Hendee, and F. L. Campbell
    1971 "Values, behavior, and conflict in modern camping culture." Journal of Leisure Research 3:143-59.
Denzin, Norman K.
    1970 The Research Act. Chicago: Aldine Publishing Company.
Harry, J. A., J. C. Hendee, and R. Stein
    1972 "A sociological criterion for outdoor recreation resource allocation." Unpublished paper presented at the annual meetings of the American Sociological Association, New Orleans.
Hendee, John C.
    1974 "A multiple-satisfaction approach to game management." Wildlife Society Bulletin 2:104-13.
    _____ W. R. Catton, Jr., L. D. Marlow, and C. F. Brockman
    1968 Wilderness Users in the Pacific Northwest — Their Characteristics, Values, and Management Preferences. Pacific Northwest Forest and Range Experiment Station, Portland: USDA Forest Service Research Paper PNW-61.
    _____ and Clay Schoenfeld (eds.)
    1973 Human Dimensions in Wildlife Programs: Reports of Recent Investigations. Rockville, Md.: Mercury Press.
Talhelm, Daniel R.
    1973 "Defining and evaluating recreation quality." Pp. 20-28 in John C. Hendee and Clay Schoenfeld (eds.), Human Dimensions in Wildlife Programs. Rockville, Md.: Mercury Press.

Zetterberg, Hans
    1965 On Theory and Verification in Sociology. 2nd edition. New York: Farrar
        and Rinehart.

CHAPTER II

Outdoor Recreation Research: A Critical Overview

Social scientists are being called to do research in areas formerly reserved for biologists. This is a result of relatively recent recognition by outdoor recreation managers that many of the crucial issues take the form of "people problems" rather than exclusively biological problems. After all, as the reasoning goes, resource managers are faced with more than maximizing fish and game yields. The idea is to regulate and enhance wildlife resources for *human benefits* (Hendee and Schoenfeld, 1973). This realization of the more encompassing meaning of "ecology" should be heartening to sportsmen, but problems remain.

Out-of-control growth of technology and population increases have severely damaged outdoor recreation resources and make wise management of existing resources difficult. This is because the relationship between man and his environment — being largely cultural and only marginally biological — is quite different from that of other animals. The problem is that culturally induced *technological evolution* has proceeded so rapidly ". . . that man is now caught up in an adaptive race *with himself*" (van den Berghe, 1975:61).

An "adaptive race" is also run at the management level. McFadden (1969:140) addresses this issue in reference to sport fishery management, though his observation applies to other outdoor recreation activities as well:

> As in many other endeavors, we possess a technical and economic capability which drastically outpaces our social

wisdom. We respond to what we perceive as a recreational need of society with a management program which changes the character of sport fishing. This change has an impact upon the desires and needs of the public which in turn influence future management. And so we track through history, trying to manage our resources to match social trends in the attempt. The chain process which sets the destiny of sport fishing is largely out of control.

Thus, the effort to gain control of management technology and shape it to benefit sportsmen has resulted in a growing body of social science based literature on outdoor recreation.

OVERVIEW OF THE RESEARCH[1]

The literature is divided into the topics (1) socioeconomic characteristics of outdoor recreationists, (2) what they do, (3) attitudes, values, and motives underlying what they do, and (4) sociological explanations and correlates of outdoor recreation behavior.

Socioeconomic Characteristics

The majority of the data-based studies of outdoor recreationists concerns socioeconomic characteristics of the sportsmen population utilizing survey research techniques (e.g., Gray, 1971; Lobdell, 1967; Addis, 1967; Bevins, et al., 1968; Doll and Phillips, 1972; Spaulding, 1971). The emphasis is understandable, since the research sponsor is typically a federal or state resource-affiliated agency charged with aiding managers and planners in understanding the needs and projecting the demands of their clientele (Dailey, 1977). Good examples of the kind of data collected can be taken from the studies on fishermen. Fishermen are found to be predominantly males (though female participation is increasing) (U.S. Bureau of Sport Fisheries and Wildlife, 1962; Volk and Montgomery, 1973; Bassett et al., 1972; Churchill and Snow, 1964; Sofranko and Nolan, 1970) who

---

[1]The literature review depends in part on entries in Dailey's (1977) annotated bibliography of social and behavioral studies on fishing. The writer is indebted to Dailey for permitting him access to his work prior to publication. In the case of citing specific studies, the primary source was consulted.

disproportionately live in rural areas or have rural backgrounds (Sofranko and Noland, 1970; Sendak and Bond, 1970; Lobdell, 1967; Doll and Phillips, 1972). They have slightly higher educations and incomes (Doll and Phillips, 1972; Addis, 1967; Braaten, 1970; Bevins et al., 1968; Sewell and Rostron, 1970) than those not participating, began fishing in their youth (Sofranko and Nolan, 1970; Kitkpatrick, 1965; Lobdell, 1967), are more likely to be married (Kitkpatrick, 1965; Lobdell, 1967; Sewell and Rostron, 1970; Braaten, 1970) and have a mean age in the early forties (Volk and Montgomery, 1973; Nobe and Gilbert, 1970; Braaten, 1970; Davis, 1962; Lobdell, 1967). The National Survey of Fishing and Hunting (U.S. Bureau of Sport Fisheries and Wildlife, 1972) reports that one of every three men in the country fishes as compared with one of every nine women. A higher proportion of all residents in towns and rural areas (26%) fish than in small cities (20%) (U.S. Bureau of Sport Fisheries and Wildlife, 1972) and big cities (12%).

Studies profiling the characteristics of hunters reveal similar findings. But when compared to the characteristics of fishermen it is revealed that even fewer females participate, and the age group tends to be younger. Further, certain types of hunters tend to be younger than others, e.g., waterfowl hunters are likely to be below the age of thirty-five (USDA Forest Service, 1975).

Though most of the characteristics studied deal with fishermen and hunters, other recreationists have been profiled. For example, data on birdwatchers reveal that they are likely to be male, white, married, above average in education, and either young professionals or retirees (USDA Forest Service, 1975). Other studies deal with the characteristics of particular types of resources, e.g., charter boat fishermen on the Great Lakes (Strang and Ditton, 1974) and recreationists visiting Toledo Bend Reservoir (Bertrand and Hoover, 1973).

What Sportsmen Do

Turning to what sportsmen do, it is again useful to turn to the literature on fishing and hunting for illustrative purposes. The National Survey (U.S. Bureau of Sport Fisheries and Wildlife,

1970) data indicate that 33,158,000 fishermen and 14,336,000 hunters respectively spent $3,958,883,000 and $2,142,648,000 on their sports. Other information for the respective categories includes: recreation days spent — 706,187,000 and 203,689,000; money spent per recreation day — $7.02 and $10.52; number of trips taken — 576,210,000 and 176,201,000; passenger miles traveled (by any means) — 29,482,799,000 and 9,284,953,000; and passenger miles traveled by automobile — 28,722,782,000 and 9,106,734,000.

These gross figures are broken down into other categories, of course. For example, expenditures for hunting and fishing are separated into amounts spent on auxiliary equipment; actual fishing and hunting equipment; bait, guides and "other"; food, lodging, and transportation; licenses; and privilege fees.

There are national survey data on behavioral patterns of other outdoorsmen. For example, the 1970 Survey of Fishing and Hunting reported that birdwatchers, nature walkers, and wildlife photographers spent 847 million man-days afield, or approximately 9% more than the time spent on hunting and fishing combined.

Within-sport behavior has also been studied. Returning to fishing, for example, studies indicate that most fishing is done in the warmer months during weekends (Churchill and Snow, 1964; Cooper, 1973; Graham, 1973; Jarman et al., 196E; Kirkpatrick, 1965), a relatively small percentage of the anglers catch a large proportion of the fish (Hendee, 1974; James et al., 1971; Graham, 1973; U.S. Bureau of Sport Fisheries and Wildlife, 1970), the most successful fishermen fish more days and stay out longer when they do fish (McFadden, 1961; Moeller and Engelken, 1972; Montgomery and Thompson, 1969), the average length of trip ranges from four to five hours (Churchill and Snow, 1964; Graham, 1973; Montgomery and Thompson, 1969; Tyre and James, 1971), and some anglers travel great distances in pursuit of the sport (U.S. Bureau of Sport Fisheries and Wildlife, 1961 and 1965). Further, fishing is a social activity most likely occurring in a three-to-four person group with family members and friends (Volk and Montgomery, 1973; Doll and Phillips, 1972; Kirkpatrick, 1965; Sofranko and Nolen, 1970; Addis, 1967).

Reasons for What Sportsmen Do

The research on attitudes, values, and motives — why sportsmen do what they do — yields varied findings. In the case of fishing one of the more significant is that in most cases satisfaction with the experience does *not* depend on catching fish (Addis, 1967; Ballas et al., 1974; Austins, 1972; H. Bryan, 1974; Moeller and Engelken, 1972). Nor does the lowering of creel limits necessarily create dissatisfaction (McFadden, 1961; Klepper, 1966; Gordon et al., 1969; Grasmuck, 1974). This body of findings is consistent with abundant evidence indicating the diversity of reasons why people fish. People have been found to fish because of a desire for solitude; a need to escape from the pressures of work, the press of people, routine, "cares of the world"; a desire to be with nature; to have companionship; to get outdoors; for peace and quiet, to explore, to recreate; for the scenery; the educational value of the experience; to have a sense of achievement; to reduce tension; have excitement; to have the satisfactions connected with obtaining a trophy; to "think things through"; to forget (Bassett et al., 1972; R. Bryan, 1974; Ley, 1967; Cooper, 1973; Davis, 1967; Hoagland, 1973; Kennedy and Brown, 1974).

The motivational factors and attitudes expressed by fishermen are also cited by hunters. The challenge factors of the hunt are repeatedly ranked higher as measures of satisfaction received than the actual kill of game. In one study (Kennedy and Brown, 1974:8), "The suspense and challenge of the hunt was ranked as either first or second in importance by 63% of the sample." Another researcher (More, 1970) described the challenge as a problem solving technique (i.e., the problem being the means of achieving the kill). Thus, "the actual kill is an integral part of hunting because it provides the hunter with information that he has succeeded in solving the problem" (More, 1970:9).

Companionship is also rated high among hunters as compared to the actual hunting of game. In Kennedy and Brown's study (1974: 9), 83% of the respondents rated this factor as similar to or greater than the enjoyment of the hunt itself. And, as with fishing, aesthetic appreciation, recreational needs, psychological release, application of skills, etc., are expressed as reasons for hunting (More, 1970: 4-7; Hendee and Potter, 1970:384-86; Kennedy and Brown, 1974:8-10).

Explanations and Correlates

Turning to the studies offering sociological explanations or correlates of outdoor recreation behavior, among the more significant findings is that variation exists in the orientations within specific groups. Different orientations occur by age groups. For example, younger fishermen generally place greater emphasis on catching fish (but are less successful at it) (Moeller and Engelken, 1972; R. Bryan, 1974).

In one study, (R. Bryan, 1974) older fishermen placed higher value on companionship as a key ingredient in the fishing experience. In another, (Gordon, et al., 1969), as age increased preference shifted from mountain lakes to salmonoid fishing in lowland lakes.

An Ohio study revealed that participation in hunting and boating activities decreased at the upper age levels (Greene and Wadsworth, 1967:6-10). These Ohio findings are supported by other research and by national survey figures (Peterle, 1961:259; Hendee and Potter, 1975:7). Another age-related factor was found concerning "climbing bums" and "surfing bums," who tend to comprise a young age group, and move away from a formal occupation as they became increasingly involved in their leisure world (Burdge, 1975: 3-4).

Rural-urban differences in fishing and hunting participation are accounted for by Hendee (1969b) in terms of rural residents' "harvesting attitude" toward nature. He notes that outdoor recreation values are supported by the homogenous friendship networks characteristic of rural areas, and that people seek leisure experiences which are consistent with their everyday life experiences. After all, the life of rural residents is typically permeated by the outdoors. Underlying such findings is that friendship group consideration may even be the prime motivator for some activities and govern outdoor recreation choices (O'Leary et al., 1974). Along similar lines, Field and Cheek (1974) report that the family unit is the most prevalent mode of participation in park and non-park settings with respect to water-based sports. Research on hunting and boating also points to the fact that family and friendship groups are an important factor in participation rates and in the composition of participation units (Bertrand and Hoover, 1973:31; Peterle, 1961: 260; Sofranko and Nolan, 1970:29).

Intervening variables obviously affect outdoor recreation participation. Opportunity and what a person is taught on the way toward growing up are two of the more obvious variables. The statistical association of rural residence and background with fishing and hunting supports the primacy of these factors (Hendee, 1969b; Lobdell, 1967; Sewell and Rostron, 1970). Another factor is the availability of free time. Significantly, costs associated with the activity do not seem to be as crucial. In a study which deals with why people did not fish more often (Gum et al., 1973), the reasons given, in addition to simple lack of interest, were time constraints and lack of nearby opportunities. In fact, the importance of proximity with respect to recreation participation is illustrated in several reports (Bertrand and Hoover, 1973:19-20; Greene and Wadsworth, 1967:2, 5, 10; Sofranko and Nolan, 1970:33). In the comprehensive Georgia State study (USDA Forest Service, 1974) it is reported that 3.4 million members of southeastern households made 4.5 million visits to national forests in 1971. But it is significant that 44.4% of these visitors to national forests resided within a one-hour drive of a national forest.

THE RESEARCH FROM A CRITICAL PERSPECTIVE

The overview of findings reveals mostly a descriptive profile of sportsmen. But the *whys* of their behavior remain largely unanswered and the variations among individual sportsmen largely unexplored. Consequently, it is contended that the social sciences have not been brought to bear effectively on the "people problems" of management. A number of factors are viewed as responsible and are discussed under the headings of premises, methods, perspectives, mobilization of effort, and conceptual frameworks.

Premises

A problem with many studies of sportsmen is that research may be based on misleading or false premises. While assumptions may or may not be explicitly formulated, they have the power to guide both the conduct of the research (how and what questions are asked) and the interpretation of results.

An illustration can be taken from motivation studies. The fact that people engage in outdoor recreation for a multitude of reasons which are not necessarily specific to the activity is not surprising to the researcher aware of the literature in the sociology of work and leisure. What is revealed is that virtually the same motivations leading an individual to work (aside from earning a living) lead him to leisure behavior. The fact that motivational research findings center on the rest, relaxation, and "get away from it" aspects of outdoor recreation reflects a value premise of both the researcher and the respondent. For most people in this culture, leisure is essentially a residual category of behavior, what is left over in life after going about the more important business of earning a living and fulfilling obligations to family and church. Questionnaires concerning motivations for outdoor recreation may reflect this bias. Such forced-choice alternatives as "to get away from it all" proliferate. The real significance of a leisure activity may be that it is *fun*, a play activity which has intrinsic value—rewarding in its own sake, as an end in itself. Put in another context, would it not be logical for the individual who places great value on his sport to say that his *work* provides a means of resting up from the rigors of his play?[2]

One researcher (Kirkpatrick, 1966) put motivations for fishing within the context of the psychologist A. H. Maslow's (1954) hierarchy of needs. Maslow asserts that human needs can be divided into (1) basic physiological needs, (2) safety from external dangers, (3) love, affection, and social activity, (4) esteem and self-respect,

---

[2]This writer has an acquaintance who spends most of his free time on the water or in the field. He maintains that one of his favorite times of the year is *between* the hunting and fishing seasons, a period when he can rest, catch up on work, and be with his family.

and (5) self-realization and achievement. People tend to fulfill first-order needs before being able to satisfy higher order needs. The point is made that fishing, hunting, and other activities can satisfy any number of needs found under the latter three categories.

Another premise which hinders the applicability of social and behavioral research is that sportsmen constitute homogenous groups. This premise is reflected in and contributes to the fact that the research tends to be of a survey nature. The object has been to gather a large amount of information from a sample and generalize it to the larger sportsmen population. Determination of the number of recreationists, amount of participation, and expenditures is used to ascertain large-scale trends for general planning purposes and to make a case for the significance of the activity. What the findings from these studies fail to indicate is information about diverse *subgroups* of sportsmen. Since the figures from state and national level studies are usually presented as averages or in other gross form, variation among the figures which might be of significance to policy-makers is hidden. To use an analogy, suppose a carpenter is commissioned to design a bed of appropriate dimensions for a family of six. The four children in the family have heights of three, three and one-half, four, and four and one-half feet. Though the father and mother are seven and six feet respectively, he builds the bed to accommodate the family's average height—five feet, one inch. Needless to say, the short bed creates problems for the adults of the family. Outdoor recreation managers encounter a similar problem when they utilize the averages or other figures describing the "typical sportsman" for planning purposes. Difficulty is encountered in tailoring policies for diverse groups of sportsmen having different expectations and requirements.

Finally, a premise exists that various categories of outdoor recreation activity are participated in by unique and distinct types of sportsmen, that each group is different from others. This is reflected, for example, in some researchers' failing to realize that the questions and methods appropriate to studies of hunters and fishermen differ little generically from those suited to hikers and bird-watchers. The result may be an uncritical acceptance of segmented

or simplistic assumptions concerning the "causes" of recreation behavior. In fact, outdoor recreation research has been typified by
concerns with single issues, as opposed to building on conceptual
and theoretical foundations (a point to be discussed at some length).
There is a tendency ". . . to relate specific characteristics of users
to a limited range of behavior, toward fixation on single dimensions of classification, and the use of novel, neither replicated nor
validated_ research instruments and approaches" (U.S. Bureau of
Outdoor Recreation, 1974, 54-55). It may be that some recreation
researchers have segmented or simplistic assumptions about *human
behavior in general* and need to link up their concepts with the
main body of social and behavioral literature. This idea is supported by the "new Columbus" syndrome exhibited by those who
rediscover already established principles of human behavior.

Problems of Method

From the review of the social and behavioral research on outdoor
recreation, at least two methodological problem areas can be discussed. In the first place, seldom is there preliminary research to
define and spell out the objectives of the investigations. Hence,
little assurance is given that even the right questions will be asked
in the subsequent larger scale or more systematic and controlled
efforts. As an analogy, the novice asks the experienced photographer what kind of camera should be bought.[3] But the answer
depends upon for what purposes the person plans to take pictures,
what the tasks are—personal slide shows, newspaper or publication
pictures, wedding pictures? Likewise, a carpenter selects a hammer
or a screw-driver *after* he understands the problem, not before. A
research method is merely a tool, and a tool cannot be chosen until
the problem is defined.

First-stage efforts may take the form of participant observation,
or systematic observations from the vantage point of a disinterested
spectator. As in any other research, the beginnings of specific hypotheses (even theories) can be traced to these initial efforts. The

---

[3]The writer is indebted to Dale Potter of the U. S. Forest Service for suggest-
ing these analogies.

second stage of the research process ideally involves verificational studies to generate or modify specific hypotheses. A key point is that strictly representative samples are *not* required for either the initial observation stage or the verificational stage of research.

In the second place, key research strategies are often ignored. For example, analytic inductive techniques permit the taking of a relatively small number of study units (people, in this case) and building a conceptual or explanatory framework around these cases. This relatively inexpensive process of hypothesis or theory development proceeds as the investigator modifies his scheme in the face of "deviant" or conflicting data. (This process is dealt with in more detail in the subsequent discussion of inductive strategy.) Large-scale survey research can be a meaningless and expensive exercise for purposes other than merely describing sportsmen characteristics, unless it is formulated on the basis of these earlier efforts. Moreover, numerous other research strategies (e.g., quasi-experimental, cross-sectional or longitudinal surveys, or case studies) are needed to supplement existing strategies.

Problems of Perspective

Research on outdoor recreation activities reveals little historical perspective. Yet, the popular literature provides information having sociological bearing on the current nature and future prospects of outdoor recreation activities. For example, the social-class aspects of angling are well illustrated by the popular writer Waterman (1971:77) as he discusses the appeal of striped-bass fishing to wealthy sportsmen. Between the Civil War and 1900 exclusive striper clubs were maintained on the East Coast. The business tycoons of the era actually used carrier pigeons for contact with their offices while secluded away on their fishing outings. The fish disappeared around 1900, and when they showed up again thirty years later, they were met by sportsmen with more diverse socioeconomic backgrounds and refined equipment.

Nor should the social researcher ignore the significance of the interaction between the sportsman and his technology. This is well illustrated in waterfowl hunting. Hochbaum (1948:481) has examined the history of this sport and proposes three periods of development: hunting for meat, "leisurely waterfowling for sport" (which came to an end in the 1920's), and a period today of "high-pressure duck gunning." Technology played a vital role in the latter two periods through the creation of better roads and transportation facilities to make isolated marshland much more accessable. The result was more hunters, overcrowding, indiscriminate shooting, and selfish competition. Thus, technology hastened the end of "the good old days" of this sport. Hochbaum laments ". . . that field gunning is the only American sport . . . in which there has been a steady and widespread deterioration in skill" (Hochbaum, 1948:482). Other sports viewed from a historical perspective might very well reveal a similar conclusion.

Another example of the interaction between the sportsman and his technology is the relatively slow development of ocean big game fishing. This was due in part to the necessity of a refined technology to manage fish of heavy weights. The sport had its beginnings at the turn of the century off the California coast, but the sportsman of average means had to postpone his participation until the 1950's and the development of such relatively inexpensive equipment as fiberglass hulls, collapsible outriggers, inboard-outboard engines (Samson, 1974:115).

The historical perspective can be used as a context for longitudinal studies of individual sportsmen, their leisure histories. Current efforts do not trace the development of sportsmen from neophyte to advanced stages. Such research would have practical application as a basis for understanding outdoor recreation behavior and serve to provide principles for modifying that behavior (e.g., toward sound conservation practices). Case-history research, whether retrospective or prospective, would yield information on the habits of various "species" of sportsmen. For example, the more or less predictable patterns of the big game fish species can be traced, but what about the "migratory habits" of the *fishermen* as they pursue the runs of the giant bluefin tuna? Do they choose to intercept him in the spring off Cat Cay and Bimini in the Bahamas, or off Newfoundland in late September? Are these anglers like their trout-fishermen counterparts who follow the insect hatches around the country? What are their angling preferences? How did they arrive at them? What are the implications for establishing the relative significance of fishing vis-a-vis other uses of marine resources? What are the implications for management of the resource?

Mobilization of Effort

Planning and support of research on outdoor recreation has been a major problem. That much of it has been local and temporary in scope and aims is linked to the fact that past funding has been for small amounts and for brief periods of time (U.S. Bureau of Outdoor Recreation, 1974:55). Lack of sustained support for this type of research has been at the expense of comprehensive planning to meet the long-term needs of many governmental and private organizations.

There is also the difficulty of attracting qualified social and behavioral scientists. Being largely located in the universities, they are rewarded by their peers for work in basic theory and research methodology and, therefore, the applied focus is lacking (Clark. 1974). Further, managers are sometimes reluctant to hire these "experts on human behavior." Managers may think that they have the answers already, that they know what the sportsman is seeking, but they are often wrong. Clark (1974) observes that this is a common human frailty, that observations, no matter how accurate people may think they are, are biased by selective perceptions (i.e., people see and hear what they *want* to see and hear), frames of reference, whom people talk with, and individuals' backgrounds.

> Real progress has been made in our technical ability to manage ecosystems for wood fiber, wildlife, etc. How to deliver the goods in the form of human behavior values and experiences is another matter. A multidisciplinary approach, reflecting awareness of the ability of social science to solve many of the practical problems of management is needed. (Clark, 1974:193)

Yet, fish and game organizations have been slow to encourage social scientist memberships. It is noteworthy that the American Fisheries

Society, since "broadening its scope" in 1888 from promoting the cause of fish culture ". . . to include all questions of a scientific and economic character that pertained to fish" (Seaman, 1974:24), still does not officially recognize the potential contributions of sociologists.

Conceptual Frameworks

Sociological information about diverse groups of people, regardless of the context, can be generalized through the development of typologies (i.e., systems of classification) based on some kind of conceptual framework. "Any science calls for a system of classification, or the multiplicity of facts will conceal such orderly pattern as underlies them."[4] Yet the development of social and behavioral research on outdoor recreation behavior often proceeds in an uncoordinated fashion. Without a conceptual framework to guide these efforts, a meaningful synthesis of the diverse findings is difficult.

Hendee's (1969a:253) work concerning "appreciative" versus "consumptive" uses of wildlife resources is a step in the direction of conceptual framework-typology formulation. He compares the respective types of users to establish the diversity of needs and benefits of each and to reveal the conflict created by their opposing orientations to recreation. He further proposes a continuum of general versus specific recreational motives, making the case that "the most appropriate criterion of equity is that priority in use be given to those users motivated by the more specific motives" (Harry et al., 1972). Subsequently, Hendee, Gale, and Catton (1971:29-30) developed a typology of preferred activities from a list totaling twenty-six recreational activities—appreciative-symbolic, extractive-symbolic, passive free play, sociable learning, and active-expressive. Further explication is not necessary at this point for our purposes, but what is important here is that the conceptual base utilized by Hendee, et al., is founded on his earlier concepts of "appreciative-

---

[4]This is a statement by the *biologist* Hilary B. Moore (1974:578, "Marine Ecology," in A. J. McClane (ed.), McClane's New Standard Fishing Encyclopedia, New York: Holt, Rinehart, and Winston.

consumptive" activities and general-specific motivations. These frameworks serve as building blocks for future research into recreation participation variables.

Another example of typological and conceptual development is the work by Ditton, et al. (1975). Ditton's typologies concern water-based recreation types and are derived from a cluster analysis taking into account the activity, frequency of the activity, and environmental variables.

Of course, there are impressionistic classifications as well. For example, Bourjaily (1967:16-17) characterized hunters in terms of the game they sought—romantic-esthete duck hunter, boisterous sport-pheasant hunter, fastidious type-quail hunter, table hunter-rabbit hunter, American traditionalist-squirrel hunter, big game-deer hunter, the shooter-dove and snipe hunter, and the adventurist-grouse and woodcock hunter. Such typologies which are not based on systematic research procedures and are not guided by conceptual frameworks are of rather limited utility, of course. But the point to be made (and that which will be developed in the next section of this report) is that for research to be useful, for the body of findings to have meaning, for the evidence to be cumulative so that scientists can indeed stand on the shoulders of their peers, research must be guided by conceptual and theoretical "maps." The strength of the conceptual approach, furthermore, is that principles can be generalized to a number of settings and situations, and complement other frameworks.

REFERENCES

Addis, J. T.
   1967 Analysis of the characteristics and distribution of the Ohio fishermen population by means of a mail questionnaire. Federal Aid-Fish Wildlife Project, F-29-4-6, Job 4, Columbus, Ohio: Ohio Division of Wildlife.
Austins, Donald C.
   1972 Recreational Salmon (Salmo Salar L.) Fishing on the Miramichi Crown Reserve Waters: A Socioeconomic Study, M. S. thesis, Univ. of New Brunswick, Fredericton.
Ballas, James A., Ann Williams, Kitty K. Dick, and C. Jack Gilchrist
   1974 "Trout fishermen in Gallatin Canyon: motives and perspectives on quality." Paper presented at the American Fisheries Society Meeting, Symposium on Human Behavior Aspects of Fishery Management, Honolulu.

Bassett, John R., Beverly L. Driver, and Richard M. Schreyer
  1972 User Study: Characteristics and attitudes, Michigan's Au Sable River, Rogers City, Mich.: Northeast Michigan Regional Planning and Development Commission.
Bertrand, Alvin L. and James G. Hoover
  1973 Toledo Bend Reservoir: A Study of User Characteristics, patterns, and preferences, Bulletin 675, Louisiana State University and Agricultural and Mechanical College.
Bevins, Malcolm I., Robert S. Bond, Thomas J. Corcoran, Kenneth D. McIntosh, and Richard J. McNeil
  1968 Characteristics of hunters and fishermen in six northeastern states. Bulletin 656, University Vt. Agric. Exp. Station, Burlington, Vt: Northeast Regional Research Publication.
Bourjaily, Vance
  1967 "You can tell a hunter by what he hunts." National Wildlife 5 (6): 15-17.
Braaten, Duane Old
  1970 Characteristics and angling desires of western Washington trout anglers, and a simulation of the fishery-management system so as to optimize angler enjoyment. Ph.D. dissertation, University of Washington, Seattle, Wash.
Bryan, Hobson
  1974 "Spring-stream flyfishermen: management implications of a specialized leisure subculture." Paper presented at the American Fisheries Society Meeting, Symposium on Human Behavior Aspects of Fishery Management, Honolulu.
Bryan, Richard C.
  1974 The Dimensions of a Salt-water Sport Fishing Trip or What Do People Look For in a Fishing Trip Besides Fish? PAC/T-74-1. Vancouver: Fisheries and Marine Service, Southern Operations Branch, Pacific Region.
Burdge, Rabel J.
  1975 Response by Discussant: Leisure Section, 1975 Annual Meeting of the Southern Sociological Society, Washington, D.C.
Churchill, Warren, and Howard Snow
  1964 Characteristics of the sport fishery in some northern Wisconsin lakes. Technical Bulletin 32, Madison, Wisc.: Wisconsin Conservation Department.
Clark, Roger N.
  1974 "Social science, social scientists, and wildlife management." Thirty-eighth Federal-Provincial Wildlife Conference Transactions.
Cooper, Billie R.
  1973 Factors affecting the quality of the recreation experience for trout fishermen at Meramec Spring Park, M. S. thesis, University of Missouri, Columbia, Missouri.
Dailey, Thomas E.
  1977 Research on Recreational and Management Aspects of Sport Fishing: An Annotated Bibliography. Seattle: USDA Forest Service Recreation Research Project, Pacific Northwest Forest and Range Experiment Station.
Davis, William C.
  1962 Values of hunting and fishing in Arizona, 1960. Special Study 21, Bureau of Public Research, University of Arizona, Tucson, Ariz.

1967 Values of Hunting and Fishing in Arizona in 1966. College of Business and Public Administration, University of Arizona, Tucson, Ariz.

Ditton, R. B., T. L. Goodale, and P. K. Johnsen
1973 "A cluster analysis of activity, frequency, and environmental variables to identify water-based recreation types." Journal of Leisure Research 7 (4) : 282-95.

Doll, G. Fred, and Clynn Phillips
1972 Wyoming's hunting and fishing resources, 1970. Federal Aid-Fish Wildlife Project FW-15-R-1, Division of Business and Economic Research, College of Commerce, University of Wyoming, Laramie, Wyom.

Field, Donald, and Neil H. Cheek, Jr.
1974 A Basis for Assessing Differential Participation in Water-Based Recreation. Water Resources Bulletin, Vol. 10, 6:1218-1228.

Gordon, C. Douglas, D. W. Chapman, and T. C. Bjorn
1969 "The preferences, opinions, and behavior of Idaho anglers as related to quality in salmonoid fisheries." Proceedings of the 49th Conference, Western Association of State Game Commissioners 49:98-114.

Graham, Richard J.
1973 Fisherman Use and Fish Harvest on the Gallatin River, Montana. MSU-NSF Gallatin Canyon Study, Res. Monogr. 5, Cent. Interdisciplinary Study, Montana State University, Bozeman, Montana.

Grasmuck, James H.
1974 The Effects of Reducing Trout Bag Limits on Fisherman Use. Fed. Aid. Wildlife Project F-22-R-14, Job C-10, Santa Fe, N.M.: New Mexico Department of Game and Fish.

Gray, David Eugene
1971 Identification of User-Groups in Forest Recreation and Determination of the Characteristics of Such Groups. D.P.A. dissertation, University of Southern California, Los Angeles, Calif.

Green, Bernal L., and H. A. Wadsworth
1967 Boaters, Fishermen, Hunters — What Affects Participation and What Do They Want? Research Bulletin 829, Lafayette, Ind.: Agricultural Experiment Station, Purdue University.

Gum, Russel L., William E. Martin, Arthur H. Smith, and C. Duane Depping
1973 Participation and Expenditures for Hunting, Fishing, and General Rural Outdoor Recreation in Arizona. Fed. Aid. Fish Wildlife Project FW-11-R, Res. Rep. 270, Tucson, Ariz.: Agricultural Experiment Station, University of Arizona.

Harry, J. A., J. C. Hendee, and R. Stein
1972 "A sociological criterion for outdoor recreation resource allocation." Unpublished paper presented at the annual meetings of the American Sociological Association, New Orleans.

Hendee, John C.
1969a Appreciative Versus Consumptive Uses of Wildlife Refuges: Studies of Who Gets What and Trends in Use. Transactions of the 34th North American Wildlife and Natural Resources Conference 34:252-264.
1969b "Rural-Urban Differences Reflected in Outdoor Recreation Participation." Journal of Leisure Research 1:333-341.
1974 A Multiple-Satisfaction Approach to Game Management. Wildlife Society Bulletin 2 (3) :104-112.

_____ Richard P. Gale, and William R. Catton, Jr.
1971 "Typology of outdoor recreation activity preferences. Journal of Environmental Education 3 (1) :28-34.
_____ and Dale R. Potter
1970 "Human Behavior and Wildlife Management: Needed Research," Thirty-
Sixth North American Wildlife Conference 36:383-394, Seattle, Wash.
1975 "Hunters and Hunting: Management Implications of Research Data."
Paper presented at Recreation Research Applications Workshop, North
Carolina State University and USDA Forest Service, Asheville, N.C.
_____ and Clay Schoenfeld (eds.)
1973 Human Dimensions in Wildlife Programs: Reports of Recent Investigations. Rockville, Md.: Mercury Press.
Hoagland, John P.
1973 A Description of Anglers and Angling Use in Two Areas of the Uinta
Mountains. M. S. thesis, Utah State University, Logan, Utah.
Hochbaum, Albert
1948 "Harvesting the Waterfowl Crop." Thirteenth North American Wildlife
Conference 13:481-492, Delta, Manitoba, Canada: Delta Waterfowl Re-
search Station.
James, George A., Nelson W. Taylor, and Melvin L. Hopkins
1971 Estimating Recreational Use of Unique Trout Stream in the Coastal
Plains of South Carolina. Research Note SE-159, Asheville, NC: USDA
Forest Service, Southeast Forest Experiment Station.
Jarman, Ron, Charles Bennett, Charles Collins, and Bradford E. Brown
1967 "Angling Success and Recreational Use on Twelve State-Owned Lakes in
Oklahoma." Proceedings of the 21st Southeast Association Game of Fish
Conference 21:484-495.
Kennedy, James, and Perry Brown
1974 "Values, Behavior and Attitudes of Fishermen in the High Uintas Primi-
tive Area." Paper presented at the American Fisheries Society Meeting,
Symposium on Human Behavior Aspects of Fishery Management, Hono-
lulu.
Kirkpatrick, Thomas O.
1965 The Economic and Social Values of Hunting and Fishing in New Mexico.
Albuquerque, N.M.: Bureau of Business Research, University of New
Mexico.
1966 "Social values of hunting and fishing." New Mexico Wildlife 11 (3) :
19-20.
Klepper, Dan
1966 "More than fishing." Texas Parks Wildlife 24 (8) :27-29.
Ley, Ronald
1967 "Why anglers really angle." Field and Stream 71 (10) :109-110.
Lobdell, Charles Henry
1967 Socioeconomic Characteristics of Maine Sportsmen. M. S. thesis, University of Maine, Orono, Maine.
Maslow, A. H.
1954 Motivation and personality. New York: Harper and Row.
McFadden, James T.
1961 "A population study of the Brook Trout *Salvelinus Fontinalis*." Wildlife
Monograph 7, Wildlife Society, Washington, D.C.

1969 "Trends in freshwater sport fisheries of North America." American Fisheries Society Transactions 98:136-50.

Moeller, George H., and John H. Engelken
1972 "What fishermen look for in a fishing experience." Journal Wildlife Management 36 (4) :1253-1257.

Montgomery, V. E., and Lloyd Thompson
1969 Trout fishing in the Black Hills of South Dakota, Bulletin 100, Vermillion, South Dakota: Business Research Bureau, School of Business, University of South Dakota.

Moore, Hilary B.
1974 "Marine ecology." Pp. 578-592 in A. J. McClane (ed.) , McClane's New Standard Fishing Encyclopedia. New York: Holt, Rinehart, and Winston.

More, Thomas A.
1970 Attitudes of Massachusetts Hunters. Northeast Regional Research Project N. E. M.-35, University of Michigan, Ann Arbor, Mich.: School of Natural Resources.

Nobe, Kenneth C., and Alphonse H. Gilbert
1970 A survey of sportsmen expenditures for hunting and fishing in Colorado, 1968. Technical Publication GFP-R-T-24, Denver, Colorado: Colorado Division of Game, Fish and Parks.

O'Leary, Joseph T., Donald R. Field, and Gerard F. Schreuder
1974 "Social groups and water quality clusters: an exploration of interchangeability and substitution." Pp. 192-215 in Donald R. Field, James C. Barron, and Burl F. Long (eds.) , Water and Community Development: Social and Economic Perspectives. Ann Arbor, Mich.: Ann Arbor Sci. Publ. Inc.

Peterle, Tony J.
1961 "The hunter — who is he?" Transactions of the Twenty-Sixth North American Wildlife Conference 26:254-266.

Samson, Jack
1974 "Big-game fishing." Pp. 115-125 in A. J. McClane (ed.) , McClane's New Standard Fishing Encyclopedia. New York: Holt, Rinehart and Winston.

Seaman, Elwood A.
1974 "American fisheries society." Pp. 24-25 in A. J. McClane (ed) , McClane's New Standard Fishing Encyclopedia. New York: Holt, Rinehart, and Winston.

Sendak, Paul E., and Robert S. Bond
1970 A Consumer Analysis of Licensed Hunters and Fishermen in Massachusetts. Bulletin 583. Amherst, Mass.: Agricultural Experiment Station, University of Massachusetts.

Sewell, W. R. D., and J. Rostron
1970 Recreational Fishing Evaluation: A Pilot Study in Victoria, British Columbia. Ottawa, Canada: Department of Fisheries and Forests.

Sofranko, Andrew J., and Michael F. Nolen
1970 Selected characteristics, participation patterns, and attitudes of hunters and fishermen in Pennsylvania. Bulletin 770, University Park, Penn.: Agricultural Experiment Station, College of Agriculture, Pennsylvania State University.
1972 "Early life experiences and adult sport participation." Journal of Leisure Research 4 (1) :6-18.

Spaulding, Irving A.
1971 Occupation, Recreation and Phasic Commutation: Selected Rhode Island Sport Fishermen. Bulletin 495, Kingston: Agricultural Experiment Station, Rhode Island.

Strang, William A., and Robert B. Ditton
1974 "Charter fishing on Lake Michigan: A survey and analysis." Paper presented at Symposium on Human Behavior Aspects of Fishery Management, Honolulu, Hawaii.

Tyre, Gary L., and George A. James
1971 Length and Rate of Individual Participation in Various Activities on Recreation Sites and Areas. Research Note SE-161, Asheville, NC: USDA Forest Service, Southeast Forest Experiment Station.

U.S. Bureau of Outdoor Recreation
1974 Outdoor Recreation Research Needs Workshop, Harpers Ferry, W.Va.: U.S. Department of the Interior.

U.S. Bureau of Sport Fisheries and Wildlife
1972 National Survey of Fishing and Hunting. Resource Publication 95. Washington, D.C.: Fish and Wildlife Service, U.S. Department of Interior.
1970 National Survey of Fishing and Hunting. Resource Publication 95. Washington, D.C.: Fish and Wildlife Service, U.S. Department of Interior.
1965 National Survey of Fishing and Hunting. Research Publication 27. Washington, D.C.: Fish and Wildlife Service, U.S. Department of Interior.
1962 "Sport fishing — today and tomorrow." Study Report 7, Washington, D.C.: Outdoor Recreation Resources Review Commission.
1961 1960 National Survey of Fishing and Hunting. Circ. 120, Fish and Wildlife Service, Washington, D.C.: U.S. Department of Interior.

USDA Forest Service
1975 The Nation's Renewable Resources — An Assessment. Washington, D.C.: Forest Service.

USDA Forest Service, Southern Region Number 8
1974 Economic Survey of Wildlife Recreation. Georgia State University, Atlanta: Environmental Research Group.

van den Berghe, Pierre L.
1975 Man in Society: A Biosocial View. New York: Elsevier.

Volk, A. A., and V. E. Montgomery
1973 The Economic Impact of Sport Fishing in South Dakota, 1972 With Notes on Angler Traits. Fed. Aid-Fish Wildlife Prog, F-21-R-7 & 8, Business Research Bureau, School of Business, University of South Dakota, Vermillion, S.D.

Waterman, Charles F.
1971 The Fisherman's World. New York: Random House.

CHAPTER III

Recreational Specialization and Trout Fishermen: A Conceptual Approach

In this section is reported the development of a conceptual approach to deal with variability among recreationists.[1] The framework is focused around the concept "recreational specialization" and is derived from a four-summer study of trout fishermen in the Intermountain West. The section includes a discussion of the sociological perspective of "leisure social worlds" as a context for the analysis, the specific objectives of the research as related to the recreational specialization variable, the results leading to a typology of trout fishermen, and a concluding discussion.

Researchers are pointing to evidence that individuals can center their lives around leisure activities as well as work. In fact, as Roberts (1970:25) notes, ". . . it can be argued that for many people leisure has now become such a central and dominant part of their lives that it is their behavior and attitudes towards work that are determined by their leisure rather than the other way around." He hypothesizes that self-concepts can be shaped by leisure activity. Related to this notion is Shibutani's (1955) concept of "social world" reference groups, which come into existence with the de-

[1] Preliminary narrative versions of this report were presented to the 1974 American Fisheries Society Meetings in Honolulu, the 1975 Southwestern Sociological Association Meetings in San Antonio, and the 1975 Southern Sociological Meetings in Washington, D.C. In this section the data on which previous versions were based are included. This represents an up-dated interpretation of the results as they relate to the proposed conceptual framework. The report appears in the *Journal of Leisure Research* 9 (3), 1977.

velopment of specialized communication channels. Devall (1973) elaborates on *leisure* social worlds in surfing and mountaineering. Leisure social groups are major sources of orientation and reward for members, just as the workplace meets the primary needs of others. What may well be significant about these groups is that they not only serve as standards of reference for leisure behavior, but may revolve around and influence central life interests and most other areas of life activity.

But all or even most of a given recreational group are *not* members of its social world segment. A broad range of orientations and behaviors attends any recreational activity. In fact, as has been noted, a major weakness of past research efforts has been the assumption of sportsmen group homogeneity, with variations among individual sportsmen remaining largely unexplored (Bryan, 1976).

In the research reported here a leisure social world of sportfishermen is explored. Other types of fishermen who do not belong to this group are investigated for comparative purposes. The object is the development of a conceptual framework, covering a broad spectrum of angler types, utilizing the variable "recreational specialization." The ramifications of leisure value systems and behavior are explored as they relate to the specialization variable among trout fishermen. More generally, the thesis is examined that the specialization dimension is a significant variable in understanding the behavior and attitudes of these sportsmen. A primary objective of this research was to develop explanatory principles of recreational behavior based on leisure commitment and specialization and to propose propositions for testing under controlled conditions. It is contended that the associated conceptual framework will have significant implications for outdoor recreation management.

Recreational Specialization

The term "recreational specialization" as used here refers to a continuum of behavior from the general to the particular, reflected by equipment and skills used in the sport and activity setting preferences. In other words, the dictionary definition of specialization applies. At one end of the continuum is the person who devotes or

limits interest to some special branch of the sport. At the other end
is the person who has more general recreational interests. In short,
the research sets out to explore the idea that trout fishermen can
be arranged along a specialization continuum which is linked to the
diverse sportsmen preferences and behavior.

Though within-sport variability has been dealt with in the literature, particularly with regard to trends within a given sport, satis-
factory treatment of the underlying processes accounting for the
variability is lacking. Devall (1973:57) recognizes this in his work
in pointing to the need for theoretical elaboration in regard to the
career patterns and social-psychological meanings of leisure activities. Thus, the emphasis here is on the exploration of the variation
among sportsmen in terms of an activity's meaning to the individual
and his resulting behavior.[2]

Variable meanings of leisure activities have been treated by several researchers (e.g., Havighurst, 1957; Faunce, 1963; Kando and
Summers, 1971; Parker, 1971). Among the distinctions in meaning
is whether a sport involves active participants in an outdoor setting
(McIntosh 1963:44). Outdoor sports in general are characterized as
"conquest sports." Challenge is provided by the environment or
situation, not directly by other people opponents. Obvious examples would be backpacking, skiing, sailing, surfing. Devall (1973:
53) notes that in surfing and mountaineering ". . . the essence of
the activity is that some people begin to define certain aspects of the
natural environment as appropriate for expressive, play activities."
But such sports may evolve into competitive activity with people opponents at least for *some* of the participants. Skiing, sailing, and
fishing[3] are cases in point.

The Case of Trout Fishermen

Turning specifically to the topic of this research, in accounting
for variations *within* a leisure sphere, Kelly (1974) views recreation-

---

[2]This is in keeping with Kando's (1975:93) statement that "the sociology of
leisure deals with certain types of meaning that activity may have, rather than
a specific category of activities."

[3]An example is tournament bass fishing, where the appeal of this sport has
been analyzed as a status-achieving activity (Bryan, 1974).

al activity as a lifelong process of leisure socialization and advocates a "developmental approach to leisure careers." By inference, people approach their sports or hobbies differently, depending on their "stage of development" in the activity. In the research reported here the idea is explored that fishermen can be arranged along a continuum of experience and commitment to the sport, from the beginning recreationist to the specialist, that distinctively different preferences and behavior attend sportsmen at each level.

The research is on trout fishing due to the depth of activity and the wide range of orientation and behavior it presents. Thus, development of a conceptual framework potentially applicable to other types of sportsmen is made feasible. This contention is supported by Arnold Gingrich's (1965) research indicating that the writing on angling exceeds in extent and diversity all other works devoted to a single branch of sport. A full bibliography would go back almost five centuries and contain more than fifty thousand entries. It is reported that the trout is the most written about fish from the sport perspective and flyfishing the most written about technique.

A contention guiding this research is that "flyfishing" for trout (a technique by which imitations of insects on which the fish feed are cast with specialized equipment, i.e., fly rod, reel and line) represents the end-product of a progression of angling experiences leading to a more and more "mature" or specialized state. Popular notions of the sport generally support this thesis. For example, Gingrich (1965:481) in reviewing the literature on fishing further observes:

> Since the kindergarten of angling is still fishing with a pole and a worm, and serious anglers generally agree that the progressive education of an angler culminates in stream fishing with a fly, it is only natural that the highest reaches of the literature should be concerned chiefly with this form of fishing.

METHODOLOGY

The bulk of the research consists of 263 on-site interviews with fishermen supplemented by participant observation techniques.

Interviews and correspondence were also conducted with people in the sportsfishing industry concerning their observations of fishing and fishermen in the initial development of the research. Fishermen were approached as they were leaving the stream and asked if they would be willing to "talk a while about their fishing" for a study on angling preferences (there were virtually no refusals). While interviews were informal and flexible, they followed a preplanned design to obtain information concerning beliefs, attitudes, values, and ideologies connected with the sport of fishing and its place in the individual's life. Questions were posed concerning: (1) fishing preferences, (2) orientation toward the stream resource, (3) history of interest and activity in the sport, and (4) relationship of the leisure activity to other areas of life (family, career, other leisure activities).

Supplementary information was derived from participant observation on the streams and around such traditional fishermen hangouts as campgrounds, tackle stores, bars, and eating places. On-stream observations included skill displayed, techniques used, and social setting. Away-from-the-stream observations focused on interactions with friends, tackle purchasing habits, and related activity.

Interviews were undertaken on eight sites over a four-summer period: Silver Creek near Hailey, Idaho; Henry's Fork on the Snake River near Last Chance, Idaho; Big Spring Creek near Lewistown, Montana; Armstrong Spring Creek near Livingston, Montana; Poindexter Slough near Dillon, Montana; Firehole River in Yellowstone Park, Wyoming; Madison River near Ennis, Montana, and Yellowstone River near Gardinar, Montana.

The strategy was to select a variety of stream types and settings to attract a full range of fishermen types. To insure that the most specialized of fishermen would be selected, a large number of streams appealing to flyfishermen were included. Other sites were selected on the basis of their general fishing fame (as established by McClane, 1965, and Brooks, 1966), thus appealing to a wider variety of fishermen. The sites were not intended to be proportionally representative of all waters available to trout fishermen. Nor was an attempt made to draw proportional samples of anglers.

Analytic inductive reasoning requires only that the entire range of the variable being investigated is present. The purpose of the research is to develop a conceptual framework, rather than to determine from a probability sample, survey design how many of each type of recreationist there are in the sportsmen population, or to make other inferences about the angling population at large. This strategy stems from the contention that the virtual absence of such conceptual framework building efforts to guide research is partially responsible for the many uncoordinated and sometimes unproductive studies in the human dimensions of fish and wildlife area (Bryan, 1976).

The intent of the discussion to follow is to compare and contrast fishermen categories and to detail trends in the data. The resulting "ideal types" serve as a basis for the conceptual framework from which propositions are proposed for controlled testing. Frequencies and percentages of response to specific areas of inquiry are presented in Table 1.

FINDINGS

An overview of the results suggests a fishermen typology based on degree of specialization. This is reflected by amount of participation and technique and setting preferences. The types are:

1. Occasional Fishermen—those who fish infrequently because they are new to the activity and have not established it as a regular part of their leisure, or because it simply has not become a major interest.

2. Generalists—fishermen who have established the sport as a regular leisure activity and use a variety of techniques.

3. Technique Specialists—anglers who specialize in a particular method, largely to the exclusion of other techniques.

4. Technique-Setting Specialists—highly committed anglers who specialize in method and have distinct preferences for specific water types on which to practice the activity.

Table 1. Fishermen Types and Responses to Specialization Variables

FISHERMEN CHARACTERISTICS	FISHERMEN TYPES							
	Occasional (N=48)		Generalists (N=70)		Technique Specialists (N=63)		Tech-Setting Specialists (N=82)	
	%	(No.)	%	(No.)	%	(No.)	%	(No.)
Equipment Preference								
No preference	44	(21)	21	(15)	—	—	—	—
Spin-casting	23	(11)	33	(23)	—	—	—	—
Spinning	19	(9)	33	(23)	—	—	—	—
Flyfishing	15	(7)	13	(9)	100	(63)	100	(82)
Total*	101	(48)	100	(70)	100	(63)	100	(82)
Orientation to Fish								
Emphasize quantity	71	(32)	48	(30)	32	(20)	20	(16)
Emphasize size	20	(9)	48	(30)	52	(33)	40	(33)
Emphasize setting	9	(4)	5	(3)	16	(10)	40	(33)
Total*	100	(45)	101	(63)	100	(63)	100	(82)
Species Preference								
No preference	39	(17)	24	(17)	7	(4)	4	(3)
Trout	57	(25)	72	(48)	59	(34)	54	(41)
"Any fish caught on a fly"	5	(2)	3	(2)	34	(20)	42	(32)
Total*	101	(44)	100	(67)	100	(58)	100	(76)
Water Preference								
"Any water containing fish"	52	(25)	16	(11)	3	(2)	—	—
Lakes	25	(12)	31	(22)	21	(13)	—	—

Table 1. (Continued) Fishermen Types and Responses to Specialization Variables

FISHERMEN CHARACTERISTICS	FISHERMEN TYPES							
	Occasional (N=48)		Generalists (N=70)		Technique Specialists (N=63)		Tech-Setting Specialists (N=82)	
	%	(No.)	%	(No.)	%	(No.)	%	(No.)
Large streams	8	(4)	29	(20)	38	(24)	–	—
Small streams	15	(7)	24	(17)	38	(24)	100	(82)
Total*	100	(48)	101	(70)	100	(63)	100	(82)
Management Preference								
Stocking	57	(27)	47	(32)	32	(18)	20	(15)
Ease of access	23	(11)	16	(11)	21	(12)	14	(10)
Habitat management	19	(9)	37	(25)	47	(27)	66	(49)
Total*	99	(47)	100	(68)	100	(57)	100	(74)
Angling History								
Cumulative	60	(29)	65	(45)	66	(40)	76	(59)
Noncumulative	40	(19)	35	(24)	34	(21)	24	(19)
Total*	100	(48)	100	(69)	100	(61)	100	(78)
Social Setting								
Fishes alone	13	(6)	29	(20)	25	(15)	30	(23)
With family	63	(29)	29	(20)	21	(13)	14	(11)
With peers	24	(11)	43	(29)	54	(33)	55	(42)
Total*	100	(46)	101	(68)	100	(61)	99	(76)
Distance Traveled								
Within 200 miles	27	(13)	59	(41)	27	(17)	23	(19)

Table 1. (Continued) Fishermen Types and Responses to Specialization Variables

FISHERMEN CHARACTERISTICS	FISHERMEN TYPES				
	Occasional (N=48)	Generalists (N=70)	Technique Specialists (N=63)	Tech-Setting Specialists (N=82)	
	% (No.)	% (No.)	% (No.)	% (No.)	
Within geographic region**	35 (17)	30 (21)	14 (9)	15 (12)	
Out of geographic region	38 (18)	10 (7)	59 (37)	63 (50)	
Total*	100 (48)	99 (69)	100 (63)	101 (81)	
Vacation Patterns					
Extended	15 (7)	26 (17)	42 (25)	49 (39)	
Short	48 (22)	42 (27)	28 (17)	30 (24)	
Seldom take vacations	37 (17)	32 (21)	30 (18)	20 (16)	
Total*	100 (46)	100 (65)	100 (60)	99 (79)	
Leisure Priorty					
Career influenced by sport	5 (1)	15 (5)	39 (15)	54 (19)	
Career not influenced by sport	95 (20)	85 (29)	61 (23)	46 (16)	
Total*	100 (21)	100 (34)	100 (38)	100 (35)	

*Percentages and numbers do not always add to total N's due to rounding and incomplete responses.
**But more than 200 miles

Equipment Preference

The proposed typology of anglers is based in part on equipment usage. Occasional fishermen are more likely than generalists not to have particular preferences (in 44% as opposed to 21% of the cases), while generalists are evenly divided (33% to 33%) in preferring spinning or spincasting methods. Specialist fishermen, by definition, prefer flyfishing tackle.

On-stream observation[4] revealed that the "ideal typical" occasional angler can be identified by his green rubberized-cloth creel, small net, and—if the water is restricted to flyfishing—spin-casting outfit with a casting bubble for sufficient weight to cast an artifical fly (he neither owns nor knows how to use flyfishing tackle). Generalists are well equipped to "catch a limit," so their equipment is marked by its functional quality. Large wicker-basket creels, wide-diameter nets, and hip-waders mark this angler. Technique-specialists (flyfishermen in this case) typically own several rods to match fishing conditions. They wear chest-high waders with felt soles to prevent slipping and carry a large amount of tackle in their fishing vests for a variety of situations.

Those individuals who specialize in the setting of the activity (spring streams in this research), as well as in the technique, are differentiated from other flyfishermen as much by what they do *not* carry with them as by what they do. Nets are not used, for this might indicate lack of expertise in playing the fish. Fish are landed with bare hands or beached. Nor is a creel carried, since fish are rarely kept, even large ones. Ownership of high quality rods is a characteristic of these fishermen. Anglers who started flyfishing with a $20 glass rod progress from "better quality" $50 rods to those in the $100 category. Or they may choose the traditional bamboo rod starting at $175. At the highest reaches of specialization, the flyfisherman is concerned with having exactly the right equipment

---

[4]Equipment enumeration per se is limited to rod type, because this was considered a key variable at the research's onset. As evidence accumulated and pointed to the typology, observations were directed to the *several* equipment items typifying each fishermen category. Conclusions, therefore, are based on impressions gleaned and field notes taken in the latter stages of the research.

for a particular fishing situation. Technique-setting specialists may own several custom-made bamboo rods in the $300 and above category and are among the first to purchase the new so-called space age graphite tackle.[5]

Orientation to Fish

Different types of anglers look for different things in the fishing experience. The emphasis among occasional and generalist anglers is on the *number* of fish caught (in 71% and 48% of the cases as opposed to 32% and 20% of the respective specialist types). But generalists equally emphasize size. For the specialist anglers, emphasis definitely changes from number of fish to size (for 52% of the technique specialists as opposed to 20% of the occasional fishermen) and then more to the setting of the activity (technique-setting specialists being evenly divided—40% to 40%—on preferring size and setting as compared to 9% and 5% of the occasional and generalist anglers).

Preferences regarding species of fish are also varied. Naturally, most anglers prefer trout to other species of fish, since individuals were interviewed on trout stream locations. But follow-up questioning revealed that the first concern of the occasional angler is to catch *a* fish, *any* fish. Thus, though these anglers prefer catching trout, a larger percentage (39%) than those in the other categories (7% and 4% of the respective specialists) express no species preference. Further, as the angler becomes more specialized, he is less likely to list trout as his first choice. The technique-setting specialist, as a matter of fact, often reported (in 42% of the cases as contrasted with 5% of the occasional and 3% of the generalist fishermen) that his first concern was whether the fish could be caught on flyfishing tackle. Follow-up questioning revealed that for specialist anglers technique preference begins to override species preference. In other words, the first concern of the flyfishing specialist is to be able to catch his quarry on fly tackle. Some flyfishermen

---

[5]Similar buying trends have been observed with regard to highly specialized bass fishermen in the Southeast (Bryan, 1974). But it is difficult to determine the dividing line between specialization and conspicuous consumption.

prefer catching other species, particularly if they happen to be from a section of the country which does not have trout fishing.

Resource Orientation

Orientation to the setting of the fishing experience, a major component of the conceptual framework, differs by fisherman type. For the occasional fishermen, preference for a particular type of water seems to be overridden by his concern with the ease with which he might catch a fish, thus (in 52% of the cases as opposed to 7% and 4% of the specialists) he has no particular preference for lake or stream. Generalists are fairly evenly divided on their preferences (31% preferring lakes, 29% larger streams, and 24% smaller streams).[6] Technique specialists (the flyfishermen) definitely prefer streams to lakes (in 76% of the cases if the two stream sizes are combined, as contrasted with the combined figures of 23% of the occasional and 53% of the generalist fishermen), but they are evenly divided on stream size (38% preferring large streams, 38% small streams). Technique-setting specialists, by definition, seek out the spring stream for their fishing experience.[7]

Significantly, the more specialized the fisherman, the more his enjoyment and pursuit of the activity are inextricably linked to the nature and setting of the resource he fishes. One explanation is that the very nature of flyfishing, especially on the spring stream, implies a close tie to the qualities of the resource. The rationale is that a key attraction for *any* specialist, whether reference is to a recreationist or to one working at his profession, is the degree of control or manipulation which he can bring to the activity. For the fruits of his knowledge to have impact, he must have a monitoring capability. The spring stream offers the setting and predictability

---

[6]Specialist fishermen were quick to distinguish between "free-stone" and limestone streams, the latter having chemical and biological properties contributing to the abundant insect life necessary for consistently good flyfishing. Limestone streams (which are often of spring origin) are usually relatively small in volume.

[7]For the purpose of this research, the spring stream is defined as one originating from springs and retaining the qualities of relatively constant temperature and volume, low gradient, high clarity, and supporting large quantities of insect and trout life.

to allow for such control. The popular angling writer. Charles Waterman, (1971:40), writes:

> It is the difficulty, delicacy, and complexity of such fishing that obsesses the expert, but it is the predictability of the trout's feeding habits that adds to the stream's attraction, for the fishermen can see the fish feed and know they can be caught if his approach is carefully correct. His failures can hardly be attributed to bad luck.

Management Philosophy

Management concerns differ according to the fisherman's resource orientation and angling preference. Occasional fishermen and generalists favor an active stocking policy (in 57% and 47% of the cases respectively as opposed to 32% and 20% of the specialists). On-site observation revealed that a frequent concern of the occasional fisherman is whether the water is stocked with catchable-size fish. Ease of access is also a factor (the major concern of 23% of these anglers). For generalists, a "good return for the license dollar" is a large harvest of fish during the year. In contrast, technique and technique-setting specialists are more likely to favor habitat management (in 47% and 66% of the cases respectively as compared with 19% of occasional and 37% of generalist anglers). Stream-side conversations revealed a concern that the wild fish population not be "contaminated" with hatchery-bred trout. These anglers frequently talk about "fishing quality" and "good management" in terms of harvesting policies to enhance the size of the fish. Catch-and-release practices are favored on certain streams if deemed necessary to maintain a healthy wild trout population.

Angling History

Popular conceptions of fishermen moving through stages in their "fishing careers" were supported. Socialization into the sport is cumulative—in other words. fishermen typically start with simple, easily mastered techniques which maximize chances of a catch, then move to more involved and demanding methods the longer they engage in the sport. Thus, a "cumulative response" is when the individual reports starting with rudimentary tackle (e.g.. cane pole and worms) in his early experiences, progresses to lures cast with spinning or spin-cast tackle at a later stage, then progresses to fly-fishing equipment still later. Technique-setting specialists were more likely to have a cumulative response (in 76% of the cases), while occasional, generalist, and technique specialists also reported such responses in well over the majority of cases (60%, 65%, and 66% respectively). As in the case of any status attribute, one does not have to start at the "bottom" of the experiential sequence, nor, by the same token, does he have to move to the "top." But the tendency is to move toward the specialization end of the continuum over time.

Social Context

A major component of fishing as a leisure activity is its social context. The social setting of the fishing experience ranges from family outings (the most frequent situation among 63% of the occasional anglers) to fishing with peers (54% of the technique-setting specialists). In the case of occasional fishermen, angling is usually secondary to other activities such as picnicking and sightseeing. But for those individuals who regularly incorporate fishing in their leisure time, the primary purpose of the trip is fishing, and the individual is more likely to engage in it with peers who have similar interests and skills.

Participant observation in the extensive fishermen friendship networks revealed that among the specialists the activity of fishing is much more than the casting of a fly. Tackle shop, bar, and campfire "bull sessions" are key ingredients to the experience. Specialist anglers are usually in the exclusive company of sportsmen having similar orientations to and interests in the sport. The fishermen peer group may serve as a reference group as well. The opinion leaders of this angling fraternity are the highly visible outdoor writers, the articulators of the specialist's value system. The cohesiveness of this system is cemented and reinforced through frequent contact among members of the friendship network. Ties are formed which transcend traditional occupational and class barriers to mold these fishermen into a true leisure social world. In addition to shared fishing experiences, contact with this far-flung network is maintained through attendance at meetings of organizations which promote the interests of specialist fishermen (e.g., Trout Unlimited, Federation of Fly-Fishermen), the magazines and newsletters of these organizations, and personal correspondence.

Vacation Patterns

Linked to the social context of the fishing experience are vacation patterns. These patterns may facilitate or restrict contact with fishing peers. In the case of distance traveled to the angling site, generalist anglers especially are likely to have been fishing either within relatively close proximity of their residences (in 59% of the cases), or at least within the geographic region (in 30% of the cases). The more specialized fishermen were likely to have traveled from outside the region (in 59% and 63% of the cases). Thus, generalist fishermen tend to fish with neighbors or friends from work. But more specialized anglers may travel all the way across the continent to "fish the circuit" each year. Having established the prime fishing times for certain streams within a region, they meet at these times with friends from all over the country.

Technique and technique-setting specialists are also more likely to take extended vacations (in 42% and 49% of the cases respectively) than the other anglers (15% of the occasional and 26% of the generalist fishermen). The latter either take short vacations (in 48% and 42% of the cases as compared with 28% and 30% of the specialists) or seldom take time-off from the job (in 37% and 32% of the cases, compared with 30% and 20% of the specialists). Informal discussion with occasional anglers gave the impression that these individuals are little involved in *any* leisure activity. Such reasons were given as heavy family responsibilities, the press of work, and lack of free time.

In the case of generalists, since they tend to be from the local area, fishing is not strictly a vacation time proposition. The sport can be pursued after work or during weekends. Vacations may be reserved for activities requiring larger blocks of time, such as hunting trips and family excursions to recreational areas some distance away.

Specialist fishermen are likely to center their leisure time, vacation and otherwise, around fishing. An obvious intervening variable here and throughout the study is socioeconomic status. Though not examined directly, the amount of time available due to job or career factors seemed to be more crucial. Technique-setting specialists in particular had taken jobs for less pay and prestige to be close to exceptional fishing opportunities.[8] Those employed in other areas of the country sometimes made career choices on the basis of the free-time attributes of the job (e.g., the choice of a teaching career for the three months off in the summer, physicians specializing in radiology to permit extended vacations). Others manage to combine work and leisure elements, as in the case of teachers meeting the costs of a summer's fishing by working in tackle shops or guiding. Or work may be shared to incorporate an aspect of fishing as in the case of a shop teacher who manufactures hand-crafted fishing equipment. There are those who have turned their sport into a full-time business enterprise (four tackle store owners and a rod maker). Included among the specialists are the "fishing bums." Four men in their early twenties had not established a steady career or job pattern after completing their education. But three individuals left middle to upper-level management positions to center their lives around fishing.[9]

CONCLUSIONS AND IMPLICATIONS

The designation of fishermen types is a useful heuristic tool, providing points of comparison along a continuum of fishing speciali-

---

[8]Sixty percent of the technique-setting specialists and 38 percent of the technique specialists indicated that career decisions had been "in some way influenced" by their interest in fishing. As this question was posed only after in-depth interviews revealed the variable's importance in the latter stages of the investigation, the N's are small.

[9]One works in a grocery store (he was formerly in a middle management position in the aerospace industry). Rather than opting for higher pay on his promotion from clerk to butcher, he negotiated for greater time flexibility and more days off for fishing. His custom-made fishing equipment is traded for such things as automobile repairs, a piece of furniture, or clothing. Existing on a semi-barter system, he pays little income tax, lives frugally, and manages to fish most days of the season.

zation. It is not contended that the framework is definitive. The fact of most generalists being from within the region may indicate that their preference for trout over other species is part of the local value system. It is not much that they have chosen to specialize in the trout, but more likely that they lack familiarity with other species. This contrasts with the specialists who have had a variety of angling experiences with different species in various locales.

Difficulties are encountered at times in distinguishing between technique specialists and technique-setting specialists and the former sometimes specialize in flyfishing as a technique almost to the degree of the latter. A critical dimension operating at all levels, but especially at the upper end of the typology is degree of commitment to the activity: the extent of the individual's time and effort investments in the sport. Thus, distinctions between types are sometimes blurred by disproportionate commitment in a particular category. Further, flyfishermen sometimes specialize in areas other than the spring stream (e.g., high mountain lakes) or they fish for species other than the trout for the greater part of the year.

Yet the consistency and direction of the findings lends validity to an angling specialization framework. A summary of the conclusions is presented in Table 2. What follows are propositions which found support in the research and form the basis for extending the fishermen typology into a conceptual framework. Since the study strategy precluded rigorous control and testing of variables and constitutes a first step for more systematic efforts, these inferences are to be considered tentative until subjected to more controlled testing under varied and representative conditions.

1. Fishermen tend to go through a predictable syndrome of angling experiences, usually moving into more specialized stages over time.[10] But increasing specialization does not necessarily imply narrowing or restriction of activities outside the specialty. Instead, an ever increasing commitment to the sport in general may be found.

---

[10] Yet some anglers reported that they had been "pushed" into the higher stages of specialization by participation in such activities as fly-fishing schools promoted by major fishing tackle companies. Thus, the promotion of recreational specialization by special interests may serve as an intervening variable in the socialization process.

Table 2. Degree of Angling Specialization and Fishermen Characteristics

Degree of Speciali- zation	Fishing Orientation Equipment	Resource Orientation, Management Philosophy	Social Setting, Leisure Orientation
Occasional Fishermen	Catching *a* fish, *any* fish on any tackle available.	Any water containing fish. Ease of access to water.	Fishing with family. Seldom take vacations.
Generalists	Catching a *limit* of *trout* on spinning or spincasting tackle.	Lakes, larger free-stone streams. Stocking to supplement fish reproduced in streams.	Fishing with peers. Take short vacations within region.
Technique Specialists	Catching large fish on specialized equipment. (fly-tackle).	Prefer stream fishing to lake. Harvesting policy to enhance fish size.	Fishing with peers. Take extended fishing vacations.
Technique- Setting Specialists	Catching fish under exacting conditions—on spring streams with specialized equipment (fly-tackle).	Limestone spring streams. Habitat management, preservation of natural setting.	Fishing with fellow specialists (a reference group). May center lives around sport.

The more specialized fishermen tend to have high knowledge and commitment to a variety of angling pursuits as an outgrowth of high time and skill commitment to the sport generally.

2. The most specialized fishermen have in effect joined a leisure social world—a group of fellow sportsmen holding similar attitudes, beliefs, and ideologies, engaging in similar behavior, and having a sense of group identification. This leisure social world serves as a major reference group for its members. As a cohesive group it is effective in propounding the values of the so-called minority recreationist.

3. As level of angling specialization increases, attitudes and values about the sport change. Focus shifts from consumption of the fish to preservation and emphasis on the nature and setting of the activity. In short, for the most specialized fishermen the fish are not so much the object as the *experience* of fishing as an end in itself.

4. The values attendant to specialization are inextricably linked to the properties of the resource on which the sport is practiced. As level of angling specialization increases, resource dependency increases. What appeals to the specialist is a resource setting allowing for predictability and manipulation, a degree of control so as to be able to determine the difference between luck and skill.

REFERENCES

Brooks, Joe
   1966 Complete Guide to Fishing Across North America, New York: Harper and Row.
Bryan, Hobson
   1976 "The sociology of fishing: a review and critique." In Henry Clepper (ed.), Marine Recreational Fisheries. Washington, D.C.: Sport Fishing Institute.

   1974 "Working at waste in leisure." Journal of Environmental Education 6 Fall:20-23.
Devall, Bill
   1973 "The development of leisure social worlds." Humboldt Journal of Social Relations 1 Fall:53-59.
Faunce, William A.
   1963 "Automation and leisure." In Erwin O. Smigel (ed.), Work and Leisure — A Contemporary Social Problem. New Haven, Conn.: College and University Press.
Gingrich, Arnold
   1965 "Literature of angling." In A. J. McClane (ed.), McClane's New Standard Fishing Encyclopedia. New York: Holt, Rinehart and Winston.
Havighurst, Robert J.
   1957 "The leisure activities of the middle-aged." American Journal of Sociology 63:152-162.
Kando, Thomas M.
   1975 Leisure and Popular Culture in Transition. St. Louis: C. V. Mosby Co.
   _____ and Worth C. Summers
   1971 "The impact of work on leisure: toward a paradigm and research strategy." Pacific Sociological Review (special summer issue):310-326.
Kelly, John R.
   1974 "Socialization toward leisure: a developmental approach." Journal of Leisure Research 6:181-193.

McClane, A. J. (ed)
  1965 McClane's Standard Fishing Encyclopedia and International Angling
       Guide. New York: Holt, Rinehart and Winston.
McIntosh, Peter C.
  1963 Sport in Society. London: C. A. Watts and Co., Ltd.
Parker, Stanley
  1971 The Future of Work and Leisure. London: Praeger Publishers, Inc.
Roberts, Kenneth
  1970 Leisure. London: Longman.
Shibutani, Tamotsu
  1955 "Reference groups as perspectives." American Journal of Sociology 60
       (May) :562-69.
Waterman, Charles F.
  1971 The Fisherman's World. New York: Random House.

CHAPTER IV

Theoretical Antecedents of Outdoor Recreation Behavior and Inductive Methodology

Outdoor recreation researchers have made much over the necessity of deriving theories of recreation behavior. In fact, a great deal of effort has been expended to develop motivational theories in particular. Researchers with a psychological orientation look for the meaning of a particular activity for the individual, what type of appeal it has, whether it results in "tension reduction," rest from the rigors of the workplace, etc. Those with more of a sociological or macro-level orientation emphasize such variables as the importance of the family and peers in the selection and continuation of various forms of outdoor recreation and its social benefits. Yet much of this research seems to ignore the basic and well established behavioral principles which underlie literally *any* human activity. A brief overview of some of these perspectives and their application to recreation behavior places the findings of this report in a larger theoretical context.

BEHAVIORISM

The basic concepts of the operant conditioning paradigm of social learning theory, or behaviorism, are premised on the desirability of examining the objective or *observable* components of human behavior. Such intervening variables as mental or neurological processes and motivation always must be inferred from behavior, so they are not dealt with. This strategy is in recognition of the long history of gaps and inconsistencies between such constructs as attitudes or beliefs and actual behavior. Though the existence of such internal factors is not denied—and though theories of internal processing are useful adjuncts to behavioral theory in ascertaining what is rewarding to the subject and what is not—such factors are simply excluded as variables in the paradigm.

Social learning or reinforcement theory explains that behavior is learned as follows: "When a response . . . is followed by a reinforcer, the result will be an increase in the probability that this response will occur again under similar circumstances" (Lafrancois, 1972:97). Further, the reinforcer, in conjunction with surrounding circumstances of a stimulus, can come to have control over the response by repeated presentation. This principle can quite easily be applied to outdoor recreation behavior. If a child agrees to go fishing (response) and he catches fish (reward), he will likely desire to go fishing again when the opportunity arises. Moreover, if the child continues to catch fish on subsequent trips, it will be difficult for the adult to leave the child at home. Homans (1974:16) terms this the success proposition:

> For all actions taken by persons, the more often a particular action of a person is rewarded, the more likely the person is to perform that action.

In other words, a sequence of events is involved: (1) an individual's behavior is followed by (2) a reward and then by (3) a repeat of the original action or a similar action. The action or response constitutes "the alteration of the behavior of the organism" (Shaw and Costanzo, 1970:28). (The child has become a fisherman.) The reward or reinforcement is "that consequence of a response that serves to strengthen and maintain its bond to the eliciting stimulus and to increase the probability of future occurrence" (Shaw and Costanzo, 1970:35). (Catching fish makes the child want to continue fishing.)

Two types of reward can be identified. Extrinsic rewards are those given by someone else, such as praise and admiration by family and neighbors for an exceptional catch of fish or kill of game. Intrinsic rewards are those the individual feels himself for

a good performance, as in the case of the highly specialized sportsman who has manipulated his environment so as to be able to tell
the difference between luck and skill. Significantly, intrinsic rewards are usually the stronger. They tend to be less subject to intervening influences and therefore, more directly related to "good
performance." An implication of this is that since it is in the higher
reaches of specialization that the emphasis is more on the doing of
the activity in its own right, the activity becomes even more self-
sustaining.

A second qualification of the success proposition is that the
shorter the time interval between the action and the reward, the
more likely the individual is to repeat the action. He is more likely
to grasp the connection between the response and the reward. Even
if he does not, prompt reward still increases the likelihood of the
response, the reward being more basic to the reinforcement process
than its recognition (Homans, 1974:17). This is all to say that success in an outdoor recreation activity, especially if it comes quickly,
leads to a continuation of that activity, and it does not matter en-
tirely whether the individual thinks through the reasons for continuation.

But all or even most outdoor recreation experiences—especially
in the case of hunting and fishing—do not lead to "success." The
times of the "big catch" or the "big kill" are few. The question becomes—why is it that the individual will persist in the activity in
spite of the many long periods of "failure" he must endure?

One answer to the question, of course, is to be found in the various studies which indicate that hunters and fishermen go into the
field or on the water for a multitude of reasons in addition to
catching fish or killing game. To this can be added the findings on
trout fishermen which indicate that the more specialized sportsman
is not nearly as interested in the bounty harvesting aspects of his
sport as in certain conditions and challenges that surround it. But
even these sportsmen would not persist in the activity without some
success of a traditional nature. The answer to this puzzle is the
same as the answer to the question of what makes people gamble,
even when the odds of winning over the long term are virtually

zero. And that answer lies in the *type of reward system* the individual experiences.

Reinforcement can be continuous or intermittent. The individual can be rewarded for each appropriate behavior (looking for game, casting a lure), or the reward can come periodically. It is obvious that few things done in life result in reward every time we do them. But different types or sequences of reward have different implications for shaping behavior. Four types of intermittent reinforcement can be identified: (1) fixed ratio, where the subject is rewarded for every n^{th} response; (2) random ratio, where the subject is rewarded n times in every m correct responses, but there is no equal spacing between rewards; (3) fixed interval reinforcement, where the subject is rewarded every n^{th} unit of time; and (4) random interval, where the subject is randomly rewarded over a given unit of time.

A continuous reinforcement schedule produces a faster rate of learning (and modification of behavior) than does intermittent, but the response is also more easily extinguished. If the fishermen catches his limit every time out the first few trips, he is most certain to continue going as often as he can. But if he then has a series of trips with a low or nonexistent catch, he will just as quickly give up the activity. To put it in the vernacular—"he has just had it too easy." On the other hand, fixed reward schedules are less easily extinguished than continuous schedules, but are more easily extinguished than random schedules. Thus, for faster learning the continuous schedule is probably best, but for retention random ratio is best (Lafrancois, 1972:104-107). Translated into sportsman behavior, this concept might be put thusly: The fishermen or hunter who "has success" at various (but at not strictly predictable) times, is likely to persist in the activity, even when he may go for a long period without success. Such an intermittent system of reinforcement, in other words, rapidly "hooks" the individual into engaging in the activity on an habitual and regular basis.

Fishing and hunting with their rather direct payoffs in the form of the "rewards" of catching fish or killing game are naturally easily analogous to the social learning theory model. But other recreation activities are just as applicable. One needs only to look a bit more closely at the nature of rewards (the positive values people place on the results of their actions) and punishments (the negative values people place on the results of their actions). It is the *amount* of a positive or negative value that is placed on the results of a behavior which determines its importance as a reinforcer (i.e., shaper of behavior).

Thus, in various outdoor recreation activities different attributes of the experience are considered rewarding to different degrees. Moreover, the perception of reward varies by degree of specialization. As an example, in birdwatching getting out into the field and sighting familiar birds might be rewarding, but seeing a previously unsighted bird would be considered even more rewarding. Further, the value of reward is governed by degree of specialization. (The highly specialized birder would find the equating of habitat with certain species more rewarding than the beginning "lister.")

> The more valuable to a person is the result of his action, the more likely he is to perform the action. . . . This proposition implies that just as an increase in positive value of the reward makes it more likely that the person will perform a particular act, so an increase in the negative value of the punishment makes it less likely that the person will do so. (Homans, 1974:25-26)

Of course, it is not any "result of action" that is a reward, but only that which is valuable to a particular individual. What is rewarding to one may not be to another. Thus, we cannot assume that the killing of game is necessarily rewarding to certain people. Those with urban backgrounds and values, in fact, are more likely to find such activity repugnant (and may attempt to force their values on people who enjoy hunting). Or women who have been instilled with traditional sex role values may find that their culturally instilled squeamishness over taking a fish off a hook overcomes whatever thrill they may have had over catching the fish. Or they may feel that participation in traditionally male sports is a threat to their femininity.

The point is that many values are *learned.* Though some are rooted in the organism's curiosity and propensity to explore the world about him, others are more strongly linked to socially defined systems of approval. The value may be derived from status among peers for doing an activity well, or from membership in a group "to save the animals."

An important principle applying to the specialization continuum is that what constitutes a reward can change over time.

> The more often in the recent past a person has received a particular reward, the less valuable any further unit of that reward becomes for him. (Homans, 1974:29)

In other words, repeated reward results in satiation, and the reward loses part of its strength as a reinforcer. Thus, if the generalist hunter or fisherman has become quite adept at "rewarding himself" with game bagged or fish caught, this element of the outdoor experience is no longer as salient for him. He simply does not get the pleasure (reward) out of the emphasis on numbers that he used to. This helps explain why sportsmen seem to go through a progression of orientations to the sport, why there is a tendency to become more and more specialized. The generalist, tiring of numbers of game and fish, turns to the size or "quality" of the catch or kill . . . and so on.

On the other hand, if one has not recently received the reward (if the hunter or fisherman does not avail himself of going very often, or if he is not particularly successful when he does go), if there has been reward deprivation, then its strength as a reinforcer increases. To be remembered is that the extrinsic rewards (such as taking home a string of fish and showing them off to friends) are not as lasting as intrinsic rewards (the satisfaction or sense of achievement derived from catching fish under difficult conditions). Thus, at the earlier stages of specialization where it would seem that the rewards tend to be a little more "external" in nature, satiation would not occur as rapidly, or, at least, there is a need for the rather constant reinforcement of catching fish, bagging the game, etc. At the latter stages of specialization, with the shift in emphasis toward the intrinsic nature of the experience, the behavior is more easily sustained, even when there are lapses in reward for relatively long periods of time.

Social learning theory contains other propositions which account for the manner in which an individual is socialized into a particular activity and the shape of the resulting behavior. But for the purposes of this discussion the principles discussed suffice for a basic understanding of the links between socialization into outdoor recreation and degree of specialization in it.

IDENTIFICATION

The foregoing discussion has centered on the theoretical orientation of behaviorism. But other established schools of thought are applicable and have utility for an understanding of outdoor recreation behavior. Behaviorists feel that the behavior of the individual is the only thing we can actually observe, that all else must be inferred from behavior. But there are other perspectives offering valuable insights into behavior that the more mechanistic behavioral perspective lacks. A remarkable synthesis of psychological, sociological, and theological perspectives by the late Ernest Becker, *The Denial of Death* (1973), serves to complement the behavioral perspective.

Becker advances the thesis that man's ultimate anxiety is over the knowledge of his own mortality, that this is what really separates man from other animals. Man is concerned that he is just another creature who lives for a period of time and then dies. The contention is that much of what humans do is an attempt to "transcend their mortality," to be "special." Such transcendence can come in many forms. The individual can take the traditional route of dealing with his mortality through adherence to a particular set of religious beliefs, by making a lot of money and perhaps leaving it to an institution in the hope of having a plaque or building in his name, by being particularly creative so that his artifacts "live on" as a monument to him after his death. There are many other forms of behavior which can be traced to attempts at transcendence (e. g., Freudian psychology being heavily dependent on the sexual component), but a primary form in the attempt to find meaning is people's identification with a major area of life activity. The workplace is one of the most widely known and studied loci of meaning.

People identify with their work and find meaning in it. They transcend through it. Less well known, but increasingly recognized is the leisure place. All forms of recreational activity have their leisure social world adherents. And at the core of these worlds are the highly specialized recreationists who find their "specialness" in the high degree of manipulation and control they bring to an activity and the status from their leisure world reference group that such performance brings.

The point of this brief discussion is to indicate the basis of people's identifying with and involving themselves in various life activities. Reinforcement theory certainly deals with the mechanics of how behavior is shaped, but other perspectives drawn from psychology, sociology, and even theology enable one to understand and predict *what areas* are likely to be rewarding. These perspectives have a long and well established body of research and literature behind them. Consequently, there would appear to be little need of outdoor recreation researchers generating "special" theories to explain recreation behavior, or to rediscover old explanations. The specialization concept is consistent with the perspectives mentioned and simply offers a framework with which to identify different recreationist groups and their requirements.

ANALYTIC INDUCTIVE METHODOLOGY

Before turning to the findings on specialization among a variety of recreational activities, the logic of the basically inductive methodology utilized needs to be summarized. It is to be remembered that a contention in this proposal is that analytic inductive methods have been neglected in much of the social and behavioral research on outdoor recreation, that problems besetting research in this area often relate to preoccupation with sample survey deduction. Sample surveys used alone, especially in the initial research stages, are likely to be unproductive. Over-reliance on them makes difficult the generation of testable propositions or the establishment of *principles* governing outdoor recreation which can be brought to bear on a variety of management problems. If the current emphasis continues, resource managers will continue to be faced with a bewildering proliferation of surveys, their practical and theoretical utility being suspect.

Stated simply, induction refers to "the logical model in which general principles are developed from specific observations" (Babbie, 1975:495). On the other hand, deduction, ". . . the process of deriving specific expectations from general principles" (Babbie, 1975:6), implies that there are already established principles with which to work. As a matter of fact, the development of a body of knowledge involves *both* of these processes.

The use of one or the other approaches is a matter of timing and strategy. The utilization of the inductive process in the initial stage of social and behavioral research on outdoor recreationists is premised on the notion that the researcher must first make a few observations of the "real world" before hypotheses can be deduced about that world. This would particularly seem to be the case if the principles which have been developed previously may rest on faulty premises.

It is ironic that contemporary outdoor recreation researchers rest their conclusions so much on deductive methods. Although deductive logic dates to Aristotle and was prominent in Western philosophy until the sixteenth or seventeenth century, the birth of modern science was actually marked by the rise of *inductive* logic. As Babbie notes ". . . the general conclusions derived from careful observations contradicted the general postulates that represented the anchoring points of many deductive systems" (1975:31). The inductive, scientific research of Charles Darwin can be offered as a case in point.

In resorting to inductive logic, the point is *not* that deductive research is doomed to failure, inherently incorrect, or has little place in the creation of a body of useful knowledge for outdoor recreation policy makers. But rather, "an exercise in deductive logic is as good as its internal consistency and the truth of its beginning assumptions" (Babbie, 1975). Of course, it is these beginning assumptions which are being analyzed in this report.

Thus, with the inductive approach the researcher, theoretically at least, has no preconceived ideas to distort his perception of reality. A case can be made that the pattern arrived at by the inductive researcher corresponds much more closely to observed reality than does the hypothesized pattern of the deductive researcher. These advantages must be balanced by the problem of not knowing that the segment of reality under examination is typical of other segments of the population one is generalizing to. Also, the deductive researcher has the advantage of logical, theoretical support for his hypothesis even though it does not match perfectly a specific instance of reality. "The inductive researcher, on the other hand, reaches a conclusion that closely reflects the specific instance, but he may lack theoretical support for generalizing from it" (Babbie, 1975).

The sequence of events for inductive reasoning includes observing "reality," finding a pattern, and reaching a tentative conclusion. In contrast the sequence of events for deductive reasoning is formulating an hypothesis, observing reality, and then accepting or rejecting the hypothesis. Obviously, the best approach to a problem area is the utilization of both approaches in a cyclical fashion. Ideally, the researcher would begin with a derived hypothesis, modify it inductively, rethink his theoretical system, reformulate his hypothesis, and seek new observations.

Practically speaking, the researcher derives his hypothesis from the observations (and premises) of the established researchers. The investigator breaking into new ground with his own inductive observations and hypothesis is likely to find it difficult to report them in established publications. After all consensus among "experts" (one definition of science) is ultimately reached through deductive verification. This is especially the case if the observations challenge existing premises. Hence, the cycle of misleading and inaccurate assumptions is perpetuated by reliance on the verified findings of deductive research. A frequent weakness this investigator has observed in social and behavioral outdoor recreation research has to do with either faulty induction or the complete omission of this critical step at the inception of the inquiry.

REFERENCES

Babbie, Earl R
    1975 The Practice of Social Research. Belmont, California: Wadsworth Publishing Company, Inc.
Becker, Ernest
    1973 The Denial of Death. New York: Free Press.
Homans, George
    1974 Social Behavior: Its Elementary Forms. Revised Edition. New York: Harcourt Brace Jovanovich
Lafrancois, Guy
    1972 Psychological Theories and Human Learning: Konger's Report. Monterey, California: Brooks/Cole Publishing Company.
Shaw, Marvin, and Philip Costanzo
    1970 Theories of Social Psychology. New York: McGraw-Hill.

CHAPTER V

Recreational Specialization Applied

In this section is presented a selected review of popular and technical literature on a number of recreation activities. The procedure was to search for articles dealing with the nature and variability of a range of sports and hobbies. No claims are made for the strict representativeness of the material summarized, as an analytic inductive strategy was employed. Rather, the object was to look for evidence of the recreational specialization concept's applicability to a variety of activities. The rationale for this procedure was that confirmation or rejection of the hypotheses generated from the trout fishermen study could be had from an analysis of the *existing* technical and popular literature—the latter an often overlooked, but valuable data resource.

The analytical framework incorporates several variables. Articles were selected from *The Reader's Guide* which covered topics of interest. The articles were then scrutinized for sufficiently detailed descriptions of these topics for analysis. Obvious variability in approaches to the activity was looked for. This variability, it was thought, would reveal itself in articles dealing with the types of experiences sought by subgroups of recreationists, satisfactions anticipated, and equipment utilized. Evidence was also sought concerning user conflicts, which are assumed to be indicative of variable orientations toward an activity and to document evidence of the need for coming to grips with sportsmen group heterogeneity.

In-depth interviews with a minimum of two recreationists in each area examined served as an independent validity check to the conclusions drawn from the literature. Individuals were interviewed with reputations for being highly knowledgeable, proficient, and involved in a particular sport or hobby (i.e., individuals most likely to be "specialized" and therefore able to report an entire range or sequence of possible orientations and behaviors as they became socialized into the activity).

A reputational interview selection technique was employed. In other words, sportsmen were contacted and asked to name those who were reputed to be highly skilled in and committed to the activity. They were questioned concerning how they began in the sport or hobby, whether they looked at it or behaved differently in it now than when they started, and whether they could discern definite stages of orientation and development. Subsequently, on the basis of the information obtained from the literature search and interviews, a range of sportsmen subtypes was placed along a continuum of specialization. Though determination of a particular subgroup's placement along the continuum is obviously still a matter of speculative judgment without the backup of additional empirical research, the potential feasibility of the specialization concept in accounting for (and predicting) sportsmen variability in a number of areas is demonstrated.

It should be noted that specific criteria were used in the placement process. Degree of specialization, as previously indicated, is viewed as a product of time, money, skill, and psychic commitment to an activity. Thus, sub-activities which seemed to imply high degrees of these variables were placed at one end of the specialization continuum, low degrees at the other. In instances where the specialization variables could not be directly assessed, other indicators gave clues. For example, equipment utilization is a key variable. The test is whether the individual gets involved in the active manipulation of his equipment as part and parcel of participation in his sport (e.g., in the case of the fisherman who makes or customizes his tackle to fit his requirements) or uses his equipment as a mechanical substitute for such manipulation (e.g., in the case of the snowmobiler who uses his equipment as an adjunct to reaching backcountry lakes for ice-fishing). The test is not necessarily whether the equipment is used as an end in itself or as a means to an end, but whether the individual plays an active role in the manipulation of the experience (e.g., the snowmobiler who races his machine and plays an active role in working on the machine can be said to be specialized). Again reliance must be placed on the original notion of the specialist as being one who manipulates his activity (and the environment of that activity) so as to be able to determine the difference between luck and skill. If the equipment serves as a substitute for this, then the activity is not to be considered as specialized.

The general topic of fishing is not dealt with in this section, in that the trout fishermen findings are assumed to be generalizable to other angling pursuits as well. Evidence in support of this assumption can be cited from both popular and technical literature sources. An example of the latter can be drawn from Auckerman's (1975) study of recreation on high country reservoirs. He distinguishes among "consumptive fishermen" who desire to catch limits of fish; "avid, non-consumptive fishermen . . . who believe that fishing is the most important activity at the site but it is not necessary that each catch the limit" (157); and "casual, non-consumptive fishermen" who not only do not believe that catching a limit is the most important part of the experience, but that fishing is not the most important activity in a visit to a high country reservoir. Graefe and Ditton's (1976) study of shark fishermen also indicates that the same range of motivation for this sport extends to other types of fishing. The popular angling writer Homer Circle (1977) reports his socialization into specialization with regard to *bass* fishing. He writes that in his 45 years of fishing his first major emphasis was to catch consistently limits of bass. "Then, my compulsion changed from a need for quantity to a hunger for quality, and I pursued only the trophy fish" (Circle, 1977:43). Now he confesses:

> On those days when I draw a total blank, not so much as a solid strike, I'm content, at peace inside, knowing such days are necessary to the survival of all fish. And when I find fish in a feeding frenzy, I'm content to catch a couple and then move away. I have no need for more because I no longer kill fish unless there's a reason: rea-

sons like good friends, perhaps one afflicted who asks for fresh fish to eat; or maybe a young fishing companion who catches a bragging-sized fish and wants to take it home to show and eat. I remember how it was when I was young, and I understand. (1977:44)

PHOTOGRAPHY

Photography, though often an adjunct of outdoor recreation activity, is usually considered in the "hobby" category. Yet there are striking parallels between the stages of development with regard to the hobby and outdoor recreation specialization. Furthermore, the technology of the activity as it intersects with the doing of it reveals insights applicable to outdoor sports where technology also plays a significant role.

The motivations for taking a picture are varied. Photography has been called the poor relative of painting and has been deemed a most basic form of creativity. Insights into the motivational aspects of this hobby can be gleaned from camera ads which emphasize that if a camera is not present during those "highlight experiences" in life, then the experience is lost forever. We can infer that photography fills a need for security and permanence. "A photograph makes permanent our own perception of the world, particularly a portion we care about" (Taubman, 1972:84). "A camera can help you see through the eyes of a child, it is an awareness expander and encourages new vision of earth" (Netherby, 1973).

> When you focus on something you are focusing in on yourself. Photography can teach people to look, to feel, to remember in a way that they didn't know they could. (Taubman, 1972:84)

As in the case with other hobbies, photography has its technical component. In fact, though the technical aspects can be highly involved, most photographers are self-taught. Recently, however, photography is being studied by large numbers of people at the college level (Scully, 1972).

Interviews with specialist photographers reveal a definite continuum of specialization in terms of orientation to the hobby. New-

Figure 5.1 Specialization in Photography

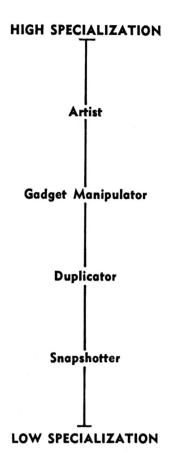

HIGH SPECIALIZATION

Artist

Gadget Manipulator

Duplicator

Snapshotter

LOW SPECIALIZATION

comers to the activity typically buy a camera with little thought about specializing in subject matter or technique. The presumption often made by the beginner is that it is the *camera* that makes a good picture, yet the advanced photographer realizes that a good picture is a result of technique, talent, and knowledge about the subject being taken (Paulson, 1975). Experts lament that beginners simply snap pictures without any particular purpose, that photography cannot be learned in this way. To the beginner all there is to it is buy the camera, put the film in, and snap the shutter. Through the technology of self-developing film, it is sufficient satisfaction to snap the shutter and get almost immediate confirmation that the picture "has turned out." He knows little nor cares about photography as an art form. The main objective is to capture something before it gets away.

At the next stage is the photographer who has some idea of purpose in the activity. It has become a hobby (i.e., a regular leisure endeavor) for him, and he may be in the beginnings of attempting to use the hobby as either an art form or, at least, a technical accomplishment. He may try to duplicate photos that he has seen or copy examples from photography magazines. He tends to be taken with the possibilities of exact representation of the object photographed, so he takes color pictures but is not sufficiently committed or advanced to develop his own film.

As the photographer becomes more involved, there seem to be two divergent directions that his hobby may take. He can become a gadget manipulator, or an artist. The former finds fascination in all the equipment available for purchase. Status and skill are determined by his peers through the equipment he owns. When a picture is taken the main concerns are shutter speed, light, and meter readings. Careful records of such variables may be recorded for each photograph in order to capture the *science* of the "good picture." In a sense, the camera and its accompanying paraphernalia become ends in themselves.

Though the gadget manipulator may develop his own photographs, the artist photographer is sure to. The concern is with whether the work has inherent interest, whether it shows artistic expression, and variation in film development is used to add to these dimensions. Technical information is digested and used relatively automatically. It is a given, not an end in itself. The artist photographer typically restricts himself to black and white film which facilitates artistic expression through its revealing of contrast, shape, geometry, and overall visual impact of the subject.

The artist photographer may specialize in a variety of subjects—photo realism (the visual expression of *things* in the environment), photo journalism (the visual expression of the *social* environment), experimental photography (dealing in special effects), and photo geometry (dealing with the geometrical aspects of visualization in photography). There is also for want of a better word "cute" photography, where the medium may be children or animals.

HIKING AND BACKPACKING

Early childhood socialization was revealed as an important variable in the conduct of hiking and backpacking activity as an adult behavior. Specialist interviews indicated that outdoor experiences with parents and such organizations as the Boy Scouts contributed to present interest in the outdoors generally and in hiking or backpacking particularly.

Hikers and backpackers are distinguished here by the fact that the former simply chooses a path or trail and walks, while the latter carries with him the essentials of overnight survival. The wide range of activity encompassed under these headings is revealed by the statement that "devotees range from the ambitious handful who trek the entire 2,000 odd miles of the rugged Appalachian or Pacific crest trails, to the millions of day-trippers, overnighters and weekenders who explore the tamer trails of parks and forests near their homes" (*Changing Times*, 1971a:46). Differences in the experience are reflected by wide differences in terms of skill and equipment utilized, with physical fitness probably being the common denominator for all but the most occasional short day-trip hiker.

Newcomers to the activity may start as day-hikers, overnighters, or weekenders. Little equipment is required. For example, the day hiker can merely don a ruck sack with a spare jacket and a little food and a canteen, and he is all set to enjoy a day afield. Such trips provide an excellent setting for mini-vacations for families with fairly young children. One can set his own pace and the amount of exercise. Such trips can also serve as a means of sight-seeing, fishing, or photographing natural scenery and wildlife (Whitcomb, 1974).

Figure 5.2 Specialization in Hiking and Backpacking*

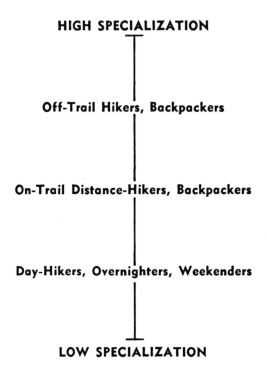

HIGH SPECIALIZATION

Off-Trail Hikers, Backpackers

On-Trail Distance-Hikers, Backpackers

Day-Hikers, Overnighters, Weekenders

LOW SPECIALIZATION

---

*Categories are not mutually exclusive since two activities are involved — hiking and camping.

As hiking becomes a more established leisure activity, there seems to be a stage where a primary object of the experience is to cover as much ground as possible, to match oneself against the elements. Yet this stage of hiker usually sticks to well worn trails. Meeting other people on the trail does not necessarily detract from the experience. Rather than seeking the wilderness experience of the more advanced hiker, his primary motivation revolves around going somewhere on foot, to see something new (Bernshon, 1973). His curiosity is the main element, to see what lies ahead (George, 1973a).

More specialized hikers are backpackers who go into an area with a definite goal in mind. The destination may be a lake, with the idea of establishing a base camp from which day trips can be made to certain locations. This type of hiking and camping is particularly appealing to families with older children, as there is a variety of activities for different members. Fishing may also be a prime motivation.

A crucial variable indicating level of specialization and commitment to hiking and backpacking appears to be whether the activity occurs on established trails or off-trails. The more advanced sportsman tends to place greater emphasis on the wilderness qualities of the experience and, hence, is more likely to avoid encounters with people not in his own party—a likely circumstance on the established trails. This individual may well be more secure in the off-trail experience. He does not require the certainty of the marked trail, does not fear as much getting lost, and likes the challenge of blazing his own way with his knowledge of woodsmanship. Remember the maxim of the expert—he is the one who likes to manipulate his environment so as to be able to determine the difference between luck and skill.

For some backpackers the equipment part of the sport is of keen interest. Obviously, the weight and comfort factor makes proper utilization of backpack equipment extremely important. Beginners tend to overload themselves, but as experience grows, the pack grows lighter (*Changing Times,* 1971a:25). Weight reduction may even become a fetish, with every ounce carefully accounted for, with every nonessential item discarded. Though hiking and backpacking are often used as an illustration of a relatively non-equipment oriented, inexpensive sport, the concern with light weight, quality equipment and clothing can make it complicated and expensive indeed (though it has been estimated that for $200 to $300 one can buy proper equipment which will last a lifetime). In fact, assumptions about the "simplicity" of the sport can be challenged by a look at almost any of the popular literature on the subject. For example, there is the article in *Newsweek* which states, "Backpackers rely on sophisticated equipment (even though they are of indepen-

dent nature) such as two-pound packs, featherweight gimmicks"
(1972:80). It is possible to compile a "basic" equipment list to be
utilized depending on the purpose of the expedition: backpack,
sleeping bag and mattress, mountain stove (optional), cook gear,
freeze dried or dehydrated food, knife, foul weather suit or poncho,
trail map, change of clothing, good hiking boots, fishing gear, and
matches.

The complexity of this activity is further revealed by the following description paraphrased from Netherby (1976:164): The more
experienced backpacker or mountain hiker knows the secrets of
hiking—to exercise, equipment, but more importantly, breathing
and walking techniques such as breathing in rhythm of steps, in-
haling deeply, exhaling forcibly on heavy upslopes, keeping a steady
pace and doing the "rest stops" (or mountaineers' "lock steps"), the
strategy of switch back on a trailess mountainside, the use of a hiking staff when descending.

To the specialist the ". . . real challenge of backpacking lies in
trying to *avoid* matching yourself against the wilderness" (Bernshon,
1973). He is not satisfied with trails that the masses use for their
investigations. He wants to discover for himself what nature has to
offer and relies on his skill and experience to choose the route of
his wanderings. Seasoned backpackers see the experience as largely
aesthetic. Netherby (1975:58) writes:

> I often think I feel best harnessed beneath forty pounds of
> of everything I need to keep myself alive. I like walking
> dark, slanting floors of pine and fur forests, and traversing
> high ridges. I like hard wind in my face and strong boots
> that feel best when I yank them off inside a tent. I like
> simple foods that taste, in shadows of mountains, like a
> King's feast. I backpack because I like to see the blood-red
> snow plant poking out of spongy brown humus.

The more committed hikers tend to be the most avid of the en-
vironmentalists. They enjoy and appreciate the use of natural resources (Fadala, 1975). Utmost care and respect characterize their
approach to the natural environment. Major concerns are with
preservation of over-used trails, litter, erosion, destruction of alpine
ecosystems (Kemsley, 1973). Since the naturalness of the setting is

a key to the quality of the experience for this outdoorsman, care is taken to enjoy the resource without destroying or misplacing a single rock.

MOUNTAIN CLIMBING

Mountain climbing can be considered as a highly specialized form of backpacking. Yet here, too, there are gradations of specialization, differences in orientation on the part of participants. Beginning climbers may take their first climbs by means of guided tours. After a few lessons on technique, they are prepared for short

Figure 5.3 Specialization in Mountain Climbing

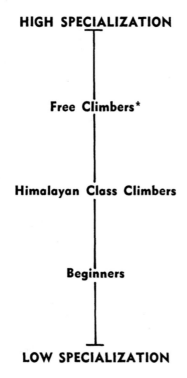

HIGH SPECIALIZATION

Free Climbers*

Himalayan Class Climbers

Beginners

LOW SPECIALIZATION

*Free climbing can occur without one's becoming a "Himalayan Class Climber."

and relatively moderate climbs. Some are content to remain at the novice level, satisfied that they need go no further to get exercise and an outdoor experience. A common lament is that these beginners typically fail to recognize the hazards and responsibilities of the sport (Skow, 1974). More regular enthusiasts enjoy the status of being a climber, as well as the experience of climbing moderate peaks and its aesthetic rewards.

Among the more specialized participants is included a class termed as the "New American Super Climber." "He belongs to none of the traditional 'classy' climbing clubs, has none of the character building motivation that once distinguished the sport, and isn't concerned with style, national competition or 'doing it for Britain' which was the spirit in which Hillary conquered Everest" (Nevard, 1972:123). The goal seems to be to get up the hardest cliff fast using the latest lightweight gear.

"Free climbing" is probably the most popular and respected form of the sport for the specialists. This involves passing a rope through successive pitons to catch falls, as opposed to using them for hauling one up. There is increasing emphasis by such climbers to do mountain climbing "clean". Specialized removable equipment is employed. No longer are pitons hammered into the walls. These climbers use existing cracks and put tiny wedges of aluminum in the rock, so as to leave the mountains unscarred (La Fontaine, 1975). This is considered as a "purist" form of the sport, with increasing numbers of established climbers turning to it. A frequently heard statement is that "there is more satisfaction because it takes more art." Indeed, at the upper levels of specialization the sport seems less goal oriented in terms of climbing the highest or most difficult peaks. The aesthetics of the experience become paramount.

A new approach to "Himalayan class" mountain climbing which emphasizes both the aesthetics and individuals' manipulation of the environment is the alpine-style expedition. In contrast to the "grand expeditions" employing large numbers of porters and Sherpas who climb in military-like organization at a snail's pace with tons of support gear and material, these climbers make extremely difficult ascents in small groups with a minimum of equipment.

> To some mountaineers the allure of such an expedition is a matter of style and ethics. . . . They will be climbers completely attuned to life at altitude on steep, wind-swept faces. They will have the patience to sit out storms, and the courage and tenacity to continue on low rations, confident in their ability not only to climb, but to survive. (Stall, 1976:11)

It is estimated that such climbing can be matched by only one percent of the world's best climbers.

Within-sport conflict is apparent. The increasing number of people participating has even led some climbers to write publications asking them not to cover the sport so "over-excited climbers won't rush to the nearest rock bearing bolts and pitons—strewing beer cans in their wake" (La Fontaine, 1975). The current popularity of mountaineering has brought hazardous and overcrowded climbing conditions *(Newsweek*, 1973). Not only is there sometimes too much traffic on the cliffs, but many of the older and more experienced mountaineers resent the younger, "equipment crazy daredevils" who do not accept the hazards and responsibilities of the sport (Skow, 1974).

SKIING

Skiing was not popularized in this country until the late 1940's. In fact, in the 1930's the only resorts were in Sun Valley, Idaho, and Alta, Utah. Because the sport was a very expensive proposition, it was largely confined to the upper class. Equipment was crude, and lifts were expensive to build. But as with the sports car, its popularity was imported from Europe after World War Two. Skiing interest accelerated in the 1950's. It became a collegiate sport, resorts opened in New England, and from there the interest spread. The topic of skiing lends itself particularly well as an illustration of within-sport variability and specialization due to its relatively high degree of organization, the intersection with and influence of technology on the sport, and the fact that it is an intensive-use

Figure 5.4 Specialization in Skiing

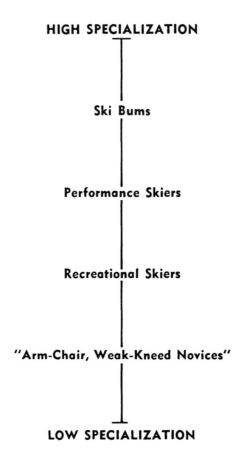

HIGH SPECIALIZATION

Ski Bums

Performance Skiers

Recreational Skiers

"Arm-Chair, Weak-Kneed Novices"

LOW SPECIALIZATION

activity. There are obvious management implications here due to the latter factor and sociologically there are implications for understanding the dynamics of leisure social worlds.

Orientations to skiing are reflected in these groups: recreational skiers, performance skiers, and "ski bums." Recreational skiers no doubt comprise the largest group.

> They . . . ski on holidays and weekends, and spend the majority of their time involved in other activities. They

generally do not live near the resorts, often live in urban centers within two hundred miles of the resorts, and are often called disparagingly "weekenders," "flatlanders," and "turkeys" by the local community. (Rosenbaum, 1976:2)

This group might be further broken down into those who actually ski on a regular basis and the "bar flies" who spend more of their time on the social aspects of the sport. This letter category has also been referred to as the "arm-chair, weak-kneed novices" (*Time*, 1972). In fact, it is reported that in this class of skiers is the individual who frequents ski resorts but may seldom or *never* set his feet on a slope. Downhill skiing has its hazardous aspects, and this individual may be all too aware of the fact. The social interaction, companionship aspects of the ski resort are what attracts this individual.

Then there is a category which has been termed "performance skiing" (Rosenbaum, 1976). Of primary importance to this individual is both the competitiveness and audience value of the sport. Included under this heading is racing, "hot-dogging" (performing tricks or various acrobatic feats), and ballet (as the term implies). These latter two types emerged from the development of shorter skis which permit high maneuverability.

A third type of skier is the "ski-bum." These are the individuals who are so involved in the sport that it may not only be a major leisure activity, but a central life interest as well. The ideal employment for this enthusiast is to be a ski instructor or a member of the ski patrol. This latter job involves patrolling the slopes to enforce resort rules and lend aid in the case of accidents. If such jobs are not available, then other jobs in the resort area suffice. But the object is to be in a position to ski on a daily basis for extended periods of time.

The equipment and consumption aspects of skiing are integral to the pursuit of the sport. For example, the development of the so-called "short ski" was in response to the need for a more efficient method of instruction for the greatly increased number of beginning skiers in the early part of this decade. In the graduated length method the student starts with a very short ski, which has the advantage of easy maneuverability. As competence increases, the length of the ski increases. Yet the skis still tend to remain shorter than formerly, even for the more advanced skiers.

The development of shorter skis has created conflict among some types of skiers. Those who continue to use the longer skis protest that the short skis (and the increase in numbers of skiers due to the easier method of learning) create bad slope conditions for the traditional skier. Large numbers of people on short skis create "moguls," bumps in the snow with diameters of three to four feet and vertical dimensions ranging from a few inches to three or four feet.

> A single well-skied hill might be covered with moguls, creating runs which have to be skied differently than smooth runs. A shorter ski is almost a requisite for skiing the mogul-covered surfaces of popular runs, as much more fast turning is required than on a smooth surface. (Rosenbaum, 1976:3)

An indication of the conflict between the traditional and new skiers is the posting of signs at ski resorts reading, "Abolish the short ski!", which is an effort both to reduce the crowds and the moguls (Rosenbaum, 1976:10).

The highly specialized skiers, as in other sports, represents the core of a leisure social world. Socialization into this world includes not only the learning of basic skills of the sport, frequenting the ski resort, but ski etiquette as well (Rosenbaum, 1976:13). Violation of the norms may lead to condemnation by other skiers, or the ski patrol expelling the violator from the slopes for the day. But a skier who is a member of the social world also adopts the language patterns, dress, and other cultural dimensions of the sport.

Though the social world of skiing is controlled usually by the more skilled and highly committed enthusiasts, membership into the fratenity is not especially difficult. The participant

> . . . does not invent this world of skiing, but only plugs in at some point of intersection between his own personal history and that of the social world of skiing. He is allowed to . . . because the social world of skiing . . . as opposed to various other kinds of social worlds, such as the world of

art, is open. If he can demonstrate, even rudimentarily, that he is knowledgeable about the world of skiing, he is a member by virtue of the fact that he is there. Only the outsider who continually breaks all "rules" is deemed a "turkey" by other skiers, which indicates that by their definition, he is inauthentic. (Rosenbaum, 1976:14)

Equipment and dress are indicators of social world identity. The specialist skiers are among the first to try the new technology, among the first to make the change from wood skies to steel, then to fiberglass, and now to a special honeycomb construction which permits the development of skis having different specialized uses. In recent years manufacturers have been turning out different models of equipment periodically, but the differences are largely in terms of style, rather than technological improvement. (Automobile manufacturing is a good analogy.) What technological changes there are tend to be with regard to the criteria of safety and how well the equipment performs. Some people are now buying new equipment every two years or so. One can equip himself for as little as $500 or as much as $1,000 or more. Clothing purchases can substantially affect the total costs as principles of fashion generally apply. And social world symbols are involved with both equipment and clothing.

> . . . The essentials (skis, poles, boots, gloves) comprise just a small part of the merchandise. The rest of the equipment is frills, accouterments, indicative of the *other* social worlds to which a skier might belong, or want to belong. Two predominant ski outfits which represent other social worlds are Levis, which represent the teenage and hip, student world; and chic matching outfits, often with ski clothes, hats, and even glasses coordinated, representing the mid-late twenties and older urban professional world. (Rosenbaum, 1976:7)

CANOEING

A prime attraction of canoeing is that it offers a versatility of experiences in combination with other activities such as hunting, fishing, camping, or simply exploring. Part of its popularity stems from the fact that a canoe is maneuverable, easy and fast to paddle, and the light ones can be easily portaged.

Figure 5.5 Specialization in Canoeing

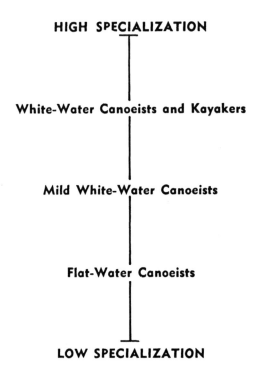

At least three levels of canoeing can be distinguished in terms of the type of water floated and the amount of skill (specialization) required. The first is the "flat water" canoeist who practices his sport on calm water with gentle or no current. He seeks the enjoyment of being out on the water and the scenery and solitude. His equipment does not have to be especially durable, because there is little danger that he will hit heavy current or objects which would cause problems.

Then there is the canoeist who seeks out flat water with current and mild "white water" for his canoeing experience. More rugged waters and isolated areas may be sought, and both equipment and skill must be appropriate to the activity. Beginning canoeists may actually get their start in either flat water or mild white water settings, and they may start the activity with a craft other than a canoe. Inflatable rafts are popular with beginners, as they require less skill to operate safely, though they are not as maneuverable as the canoe.

The most skilled and specialized include "white water" canoeists and kayakers who prefer the more "heavy," dangerous water. Their equipment is highly specialized to meet the demands of the sport. At this end of the specialization continuum white water "classes" have been devised in terms of the difficulty of canoeing or kayaking it, the amount of danger involved. There are clubs which teach the control and maneuvering of crafts so as to be able to advance the individual into the more difficult classes of water. Formal competition has been organized in the form of running slalom courses in white water (Elkins, 1974).

Conflict between canoeists and private land owners along the streams is common. There are also conflicts between canoeists and fishermen and overcrowding along popular float streams.

BIRDWATCHING

Authorities on birdwatching (or "birding") concede that it shares enduring features of other established sports (Martin, 1974:88). There is a wide range of pleasures associated with it. The activity can take place in a variety of places, and it can be a grueling, even dangerous, sport. Further, it can be undertaken by individuals or groups, or actually be "played" as a team on a scoring basis. The "good" of the sport is said to be that it provides the participant with an outlet for communing with nature, relating to the environment, and becoming more knowledgeable about all types of birds (Martin, 1974:88).

The beginning birder is provided with a simple strategy in getting started in the sport—to read a nontechnical book about birds (Small, 1973). It is also emphasized that little skill is required of the beginner, yet, that most of the discoveries of bird behavior have been made by amateurs and not by professional ornithologists (George, 1973b). Basic equipment is defined as a field guide to birds, list of birds in the area, binoculars, and a pair of comforta-

Figure 5.6 Specialization in Birdwatching

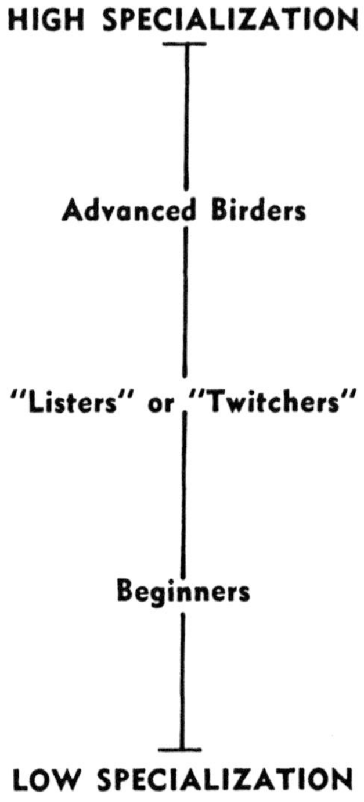

HIGH SPECIALIZATION

Advanced Birders

"Listers" or "Twitchers"

Beginners

LOW SPECIALIZATION

ble shoes. Typical dress is in khakis and a plaid shirt with sufficiently large pockets to hold books and papers (Martin, 1974:90).

Distinct stages of development have been observed even by the popular writers in this field. The novice birder is content with finding and matching birds with an identification list. He gains much of his satisfactions by comparing his list with someone else's (Adams, 1974:16).

At another stage is the birder who places emphasis on the number of birds he can check off on his "life list." This emphasis on numbers is sometimes carried to the point of entering formal competition as to the most birds sighted in a single day.

More specialized birders place increasing importance in the skill of observation. They are intent on being knowledgeable of various bird behavior patterns, along with the physical appearance of the bird and its sound. There is also a tendency to study a particular kind of bird and its habits (Adams, 1975). Habitat and conditions can be major considerations. "A *good* birder notices what kind of bushes are in the area, whether the water is fresh or brackish, how fast the wind is blowing, and what the weather is going to be the next day" (Martin, 1974:88). The most specialized and committed birders are very selective in choosing the area for study and the physical make-up of the land.

Conflicts between birders and other recreationists result from the fact that the habitats of birds are often the sites for swimmers, picnickers, and noisy children. Conflicts *within* the sport have to do with differing definitions of what birding should be. The more advanced are scornful of the less specialized birders with their "find and list" orientations. In fact, in England the "listers" are known by the derogatory term of "twitchers," because they "twitch off" to see a bird. They are derogated because they do not fully study and explore for the intricacies in bird behavior (Martin, 1974:88-92). Or the traditionalists may complain about the listers who destroy a field to see a bird. Listers are accused of even harming the ecology of the terrain by their indifferent, goal-oriented behavior.

HUNTING

Hunting incorporates such a wide range of pursuits that it is difficult to generalize specialization levels without breaking the activity down into categories. Yet, it is apparent that early experiences with the sport in general determine whether it will be pursued by the adult at all. In other words, it is especially unlikely in this sport that the individual will begin hunting if he has not been exposed to it at least by his mid-twenties. Evidence for this is well documented in a number of studies. For example, in one study (Bond and Whittaker, 1971) the average hunter, who was 38 years old, had been participating in the sport for 21 years. In fact, 84% of the hunters had participated in their youth. They learned the sport around the age of 17, and 70% were introduced to it by parents or relatives.

Noteworthy is the fact that hunting and fishing are relatively well researched in this regard, while other outdoor recreation activities are not. But there is little reason to suspect that socialization into other activities is much different, unless they are highly promoted by equipment manufacturers and/or not as demanding in terms of specialized knowledge (e.g., as in the case of recreational power boating).

Due to the diversity and range of activity subsumed under hunting, the principle that specialization occurs both within and between different types is well illustrated. If within-system specialization is looked at first, there appears to be a definite progression of behaviors and orientations from relatively simple to specialized stages. The deer hunter, for example, is likely to start with the orientation of making a kill—in fact, just as the beginning trout fisherman, any size or condition of animal will do, as long as it is acceptable to local folkways and mores.[1] The setting for the less specialized deer hunter is likely to be manning a stand on an organized hunt. As experience is gained there is more concentration on the trophy aspects of the sport, as opposed to the number of animals killed. Hunting strategies also change. "Stillhunting" is considered to require special knowledge and skill. In introducing their readers to an article on tactics for hunting deer, the editors of *Outdoor Life* (1976:61) describe stillhunting within the context of the sport in general as follows:

> Deer hunting is a parochial sport. New Englanders can't understand why Southerners call deer hunting with dogs a sport. Southerners wonder how New Englanders manage to shoot deer without a pack. Then there are the stand-and-drive hunters of Pennsylvania, who can't use hounds because the law forbids it, and so use human drivers instead. And that state's law provides that there shall be no more than 25 men in the same gang. Twenty-five men! To a Western mule-deer hunter, that sounds like an army. Most deer hunters, though, have great respect for the lone

---

[1]One particularly strong prohibition in the Southeast which even the beginning hunter is likely to honor is against the shooting of doe and antlerless bucks. In spite of recent encouragement by game officials to shoot these animals to reduce overpopulations, the cultural prohibitions have been slow to yield.

stillhunter—the man who goes out by himself and kills a deer simply by stalking. He doesn't use hounds or human drivers. He moves carefully and hunts quietly. Therefore, he is a stillhunter, a word we inherited from England, where noblemen hunted deer with hounds, horses, and hunting horns. The commoner—forbidden to kill the King's deer on pain of death—hunted very quietly indeed.

As levels of specialization increase, there appears to be a tendency toward progression in methods. From shotgun to rifle to bow and arrow would be the logical sequence. There is also the tendency at more specialized levels toward emphasis on the nonconsumptive aspects of the sport. The essence of the experience be-

Figure 5.7 Specialization in Hunting (Within Categories)

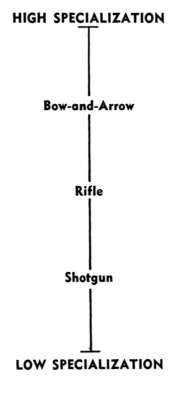

HIGH SPECIALIZATION

Bow-and-Arrow

Rifle

Shotgun

LOW SPECIALIZATION

comes less the kill and more the pursuit, the challenge of knowing and tracking the animal.[2]

If we look at the specialization dimension at the *between* (or among) categories level, the inherent nature of the game and setting in which the sport occurs seems to determine who its adherents will be. In the Southeast the progression of hunting experiences seems to be from small game, to deer, then to birds—with the turkey being recognized as the ultimate challenge. Naturally, as in the case of other sports, intervening variables are present to complicate this progression somewhat. Socioeconomic class in particular seems to affect participation in bird hunting, and there is an interesting and significant interaction between class factors and availability of hunting. Much of the land in the Southeast is privately owned, especially land that is suitable for such hunting. Thus, the bird hunter faces problems of access unless he himself owns the land or he is a member of a hunting club.

Within the sport of bird hunting there have even occurred shifts in emphasis in the past few years. Quail hunting is best in areas with relatively small farms breaking the landscape, and, of course, dogs are a necessary component of a successful hunt. Yet the trend toward increasingly large plots of tilled land has created better habitat for doves. Many maintain that dove hunting is an easier sport (and it does not require dogs). Further, it is particularly appealing for its social aspects. Groups of sportsmen can meet at a good field and enjoy the comradeship of the hunt.

Coon hunting is another sport which seems to lend itself particularly well to comradeship, and the fact that dogs are required adds another dimension, as in the case of quail hunting. Again, though this researcher cannot point to systematically derived evidence on the topic, it appears that coon hunting appeals to lower middle and working class individuals, as opposed to the appeal of

---

[2]Hunters may be misunderstood by the mass media for the very reason that social researchers have had theoretical problems with outdoor recreation behavior — namely, due to the assumption of category homogeneity. The "Guns of Autumn" television program which depicted the hunter as a wanton killer is a case in point. At best the camera attended to individuals at the least specialized stages of the sport where the kill is the primary ingredient.

Figure 5.8 Specialization in Hunting (Between Categories)

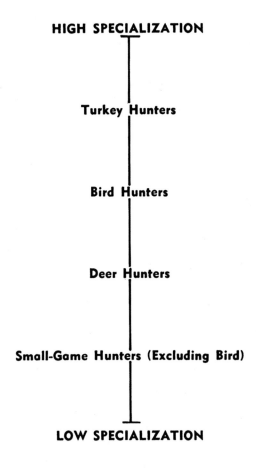

HIGH SPECIALIZATION

Turkey Hunters

Bird Hunters

Deer Hunters

Small-Game Hunters (Excluding Bird)

LOW SPECIALIZATION

quail hunting to the upper middle and upper classes. A key variable again appears to be that access to land for the sole purpose of coon hunting is more readily obtained than for other types. Further, the hunting takes place at night when the working individual is free.

As with other recreational activities, involvement with the equipment and technology of the sport can become almost an end in itself. In the case of hunting, preoccupation with guns is the most likely equipment involvement (though sportsmen can become exuberant with anything from their four-wheel drive vehicles to their game calls). Again, due to equipment promotion, sportsmen who are less specialized may be seen carrying expensive and highly refined equipment. Yet the use to which the equipment is put is revealing of the degree of specialization. A case in point is the shooting of game from extreme distances with the aid of highly refined telescopic sights (and even range finders!). Then, of course, target shooting of various types is a highly specialized and competitive sport with its "hard core" of adherents, just as dog breeding and showing has its adherents.

The sport of hunting may attract the most avid specialists of any sport. One researcher (Copp, 1975) asked a sample of duck hunters if their keen interest in hunting had ever gotten them in trouble— almost half said it had. One confided:

> I've been married twice, and hunting's done me in each time. . . . Look what happened last time. . . . I had this old dog, he was damn good, too, but by God if he didn't raise a little hell around the house once in awhile. The old lady didn't go so much for that, you know, and she says to me one day, "Al," she says, "it's either me or that goddamned dog."
> Well, I thought on that for awhile, then I say to myself, by God, you can't find a good dog like that everyday. No sir, that's the truth. So I say to her, "Why hell, that's no choice," and I helped her pack her bags. And she went. too, by God. Listen, I love to hunt, let me tell you. The reason I work is so's I can buy guns, ammo, and dog food. (67)

REFERENCES

Adams, M. V.
   1975 "Have you started your life list?" National Wildlife 13 (June):14-16.
Auckerman, Robert
    1975 Feasibility and Potential of Enhancing Water Recreation Opportunities on High Country Reservoirs. Environmental Resources Center Completion Report Series #62 (June). Colorado State University, Fort Collins.
Bernshon, Ken
   1973 "The backpack gourmet." Field and Stream 78 (July):64+
Bond, Robert S., and James C. Whittaker
    1971 Hunter-fishermen characteristics: Factors in wildlife management and policy decisions, pp. 128-134. In Recreational Symposium Proceedings,

Upper Darby, Penn.: USDA Forest Service Northeast Forest Experiment Station.

(Eds.)
1972 "Boon or bane." Newsweek 79 (January 24) :67.
Circle, Homer
1977 "If I catch a world record bass, I'll put it back." Sports Afield (June): 42-44, 167-168.
Copp, John D.
1975 "Why hunters like to hunt." Psychology Today 9 (December) :60-67.
(Eds.)
1976 "Deer tactics that really work." Outdoor Life 158 (September) :61.
Elkins, Pete
1974 "Float-fishing frenzy." Field and Stream 79 (October) :134-136.
Fadala, Sam
1975 "The mountain rock store." Field and Stream 80 (October) :97+.
George, Jean
1973a "Camping out is pure pleasure." Reader's Digest 102 (June) :139-142.
1973b "The new art of bird reading." Reader's Digest 102 (March) :136-140.
Graefe, Alan R., and Robert Ditton
1976 "Recreational shark fishing on the Texas Gulf Coast: an exploratory study of behavior and attitudes." Marine Fisheries Review 38:10-20.
Kemsley, William
1973 "We're loving our wilderness to death." Audubon 75 (May) :111-113.
La Fontaine, B.
1975 "Rocks in their heads and hearts." Sports Illustrated 42 (May 19) :40-43.
Martin, William C.
1974 "Game-time in cloud-cuckoo land." Harpers 249 (December) :88-92+.
Netherby, Steve
1973 "How to shoot a backpacker." Field and Stream 78 (July) :106-109.
1975 "Lightweight fishing gear for backpackers." Field and Stream 80 (May): 58-62+.
1976 "The way to the top." Field and Stream 80 (February) :160+.
Nevard, P.
1972 "Go and try it on the mountain." Esquire 78 (August) :121-127.
(Eds.)
1972 "New frontiers men: backpacking." Newsweek 80 (July 3) :47.
1971a "Now everybody's backpacking." Changing Times 25 (July) :46-47.
Paulson, F. M.
1975 "For nautical shutterbugs." Field and Stream 80 (August) :78-80.
(Eds.)
1973 "Peak traffic." Newsweek 82 (August 20) :49.
Rosenbaum, Marsha
1976 The Social World of Skiing. Unpublished paper, Graduate Program in Sociology, University of California, San Francisco, California.
Scully, J.
1972 "First wave: a new breed of photographer." Modern Photography 36 (June) :70-79.
(Eds.)
1972 "Skiing the new lure of a supersport." Time 100 (December 25) :54-63.
Skow, John
1974 "Second man on a string." Atlantic Monthly 233 (June) :48-53.

Small, D. E.
  1973 "What does a beginner birdwatcher do?" American Forest 79 (July):
    38-40.
Stall, Bill
  1976 "Americans gaining in mountaineering." The Los Angeles Times (De-
    cember 1):11.
Taubman, P.
  1972 "Most basic form of creativity." Interview, edited by P. Taubman with
    Edwin Land. Time 99 (June 26):84.
(Eds.)
  1971b "Tips for would-be birdwatchers." Changing Times 25 (September):38.
Whitcomb, Roberta J.
  1974 "Family in the wilderness: happiness, is a backpacking trip." Outdoor
    Life 153 (March):84-85+.

CHAPTER VI

Conclusions and Implications

SPECIALIZATION AND BEHAVIOR

A number of generalizations can be made about the role of specialization in recreation behavior:

1. Newcomers to an activity are intent on getting results, *any* results. The beginning photographer wants his snapshots of the children to turn out. The novice hiker wants to get from point A to point B, in relative comfort, without blisters on his feet. Newcomers want to "make it to the top"—any means will do. And so it goes with new skiers getting down the slope right-side-up; canoeists making it down the river without capsizing; birdwatchers being able to identify a bird, *any* bird; fishermen making a catch; hunters making a kill.

2. As a particular activity becomes an established behavior, when the participant becomes competent in it, the recreationist seeks to validate that competence with the *number* of successes had or he operates in settings providing greater challenge. Just as the generalist trout fisherman seeks to "catch a limit" the hunter wants to "bag a limit". Hikers and backpackers emphasize distance and endurance; birdwatchers accumulate long lists of birds sighted; skiers want to master the more difficult slopes; canoeists seek the white water; and photographers attempt to duplicate the results of professionals.

3. It is after the "generalist" or accomplished stage of development is reached that the recreationist seems most vulnerable to adjunct types of specialization. The hunter who has specialized in

quail may develop a keen interest in dogs. The flyfishermen may become fixated on fly-tying and entomology. In fact, preoccupation with sporting equipment may become an end in itself. In the Southeast especially, the bass boat phenomenon lends itself particularly well to such preoccupation. A significant segment of the fishermen who use this complicated, expensive, and high powered equipment no doubt enjoy the gadget and speed aspects as much as the actual fishing. The "gadget manipulator" photographer, of course, also personifies the equipment enthusiast.

4. Finally, at the extreme end of the specialization continuum are those recreationists who place the most emphasis on doing the activity for its own sake, those who are heard most frequently to refer to the "quality" of the experience and those who make the most specific demands for particular resource settings. Comprised in this category are the "artist photographers" who view the camera as a means to creative expression. Here too are found the hunter who minimizes the importance of the kill, the hiker who seeks the challenge of unguided journeys, and the "free-climber" who enjoys the form, the process of the activity. These are the core members of leisure social worlds. They sometimes center much of their lives and identities around their sports or hobbies.

SPECIALIZATION AND THEORY

1. From the standpoint of theory it is important to remember that the specialization dimension likely underlies *any* recreational activity. Yet the length of the continuum will differ for different activities and the activities themselves can be arranged on a specialization continuum. This point can be illustrated hypothetically. Certain activities, by their very nature, lend themselves more easily than others to high or low specialization, or to wider or narrower ranges. Thus, automobile touring would seem to have rather limited possibilities for a high degree of specialization. It must be assumed that the driver knows how to drive (and has a license), that some automobile tourists very carefully plan their journeys and take extended trips. But taking an automobile through a national forest or park simply does not offer the range of environmental manipula-

Figure 6.1 Between-System Specialization: Automobile Touring, Camping, Fishing

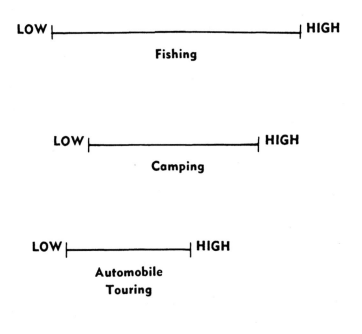

tion that backpacking the trails of a park would. Camping, on the other hand, seems to offer more opportunities. One may simply sleep in the back of his station wagon or truck for a night or two, or he can take a backpacking expedition into the wilderness. Fishing seems to offer a particularly wide range of specialization because of the tremendous variety of settings and experiences available and promotion of equipment technology.

**Figure 6.2 Within-System Specialization:
Hunting**

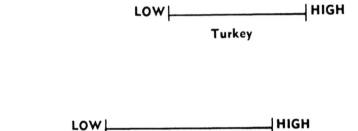

Turkey

Deer

Small Game

Hunting (General)

Within broad categories of sportsmen the same principles apply.
As was discussed in the findings on hunters, subcategories of behavior can be identified. Thus, while the range of specialization
for hunting in general would be wide, certain types of hunting define specialization ranges in themselves. Smallgame hunting with
a rifle, for example, can be considered more specialized than hunting deer from a stand (unless the deer hunter is using a bow and

arrow). But deer stalking may be more specialized than the normal range of experiences available to the small game hunter.[1]

2. An expectation would be that the number of individuals participating at various levels of specialization is skewed toward the low end of the continuum, and that different activities have different degrees of participation at each level. Only through random probability samples broken down by specialization indicators can this be

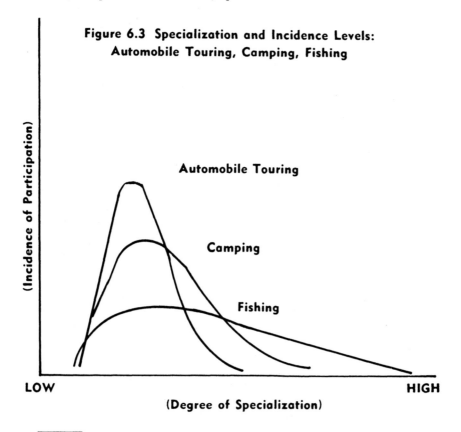

Figure 6.3 Specialization and Incidence Levels: Automobile Touring, Camping, Fishing

(Incidence of Participation)

Automobile Touring

Camping

Fishing

LOW HIGH

(Degree of Specialization)

---

[1]This is *not* to say that small-game hunting can *always* be considered less specialized than highly refined deer hunting. Doubtlessly there are small game hunters who are just as specialized as the most refined deer stalkers. But the point is that the range of activities *most readily available* to different groups of sportsmen determines the probability of specialization. The degree of refinement already existing and reflected in the literature and technology of a sport is both a determinant and reflection of this.

ascertained. Such information should provide valuable guidelines for planning purposes and would be much superior to the usual aggregate data.

3. The determination of specialization levels can be undertaken by simple observation or use of questionnaires. But, again, a cautionary note is in order. The assumption cannot always be made that activities requiring expensive and complicated mobilization of resources, such as big game hunting or fishing, attract the specialist oriented sportsman. These endeavors typically involve the use of guides who manipulate the environment for their clients. The point is that it is the *guides* who fall on the high end of the specialization continuum, not necessarily the sportsmen they serve. The former carry the requisite knowledge, skills, and commitment, while the latter can be viewed as *buying* the recreation experience. Individuals who purchase the service of guides may not have gone through the extended socialization process for the development of skills and resources to pursue the sport on their own (or they may not have been able monetarily to afford it).

It should also be remembered that equipment interest can reflect specialization, or it can reflect a relatively low level of skill and involvement. Individuals who want to "have it done for them" can just as readily purchase a trail bike, snowmobile, or bass boat as those who use such equipment out of highly specialized involvement in the activity. The critical question is whether the equipment is used as a *substitute* for skill and knowledge in the case of the novice or general recreationist, or as an *adjunct* in the case of the specialist.

4. A most important implication of this research is that the focus of outdoor recreation studies can be profitably shifted from belabored investigations of the internal motivational states of sportsmen to the behavioral outcomes. As interesting as they are, the abstract psychological studies of why sportsmen do what they do have not been particularly productive as guides to the everyday problems of managers. The specialization indicator approach instead focuses on the manifestations of actual sportsmen behavior and interprets them directly and meaningfully.

5. Further, a multitude of recreation behaviors can be integrated in terms of established reinforcement theory (social learning theory) principles. There is no need to search for a "new theory" with which to explain and predict sportsmen behavior when there is one that is already well established and validated.

SPECIALIZATION AND MANAGEMENT

1. A major implication of the specialization principle for outdoor recreation management is that managers can no longer assume that different sportsmen groups can be managed as if the labels themselves are adequate guides to policy. What must be ascertained are the orientations of subgroups within categories, subgroups which arc formed by similar levels of specialization.

The seriousness of failure to recognize that every sportsmen category is comprised of distinct subgroups with quite different orientations, interests, and expectations for the outdoor experience cannot be overstated. The mistaken assumption of category homogeneity is frequently revealed in research findings that do not seem readily explainable. For example, one such study on factors affecting satisfaction with guided Colorado River float trips revealed that the density of use (number of other floaters seen during the trip) did not seem to affect the quality of the experience. The easiest conclusion is that density is not a factor in float trips. But the very nature of *guided* trips is that they tend to attract the less committed and specialized recreationist. The upper ends of the specialization continuum are simply not represented. In fact, the hallmark of the specialized sportsman is that he places high value on manipulating the environment for himself, rather than having it done for him. Moreover, this sportsman usually places high value on the natural or wilderness qualities of the experience and is most likely to be offended by the repeated presence of other individuals in the outdoor environment. A policy decision based on the conclusion that density is not a factor in the perceived quality of the outdoor experience would doubtlessly cause much resistance by organized groups of specialists who do not have the experience "done for them" by guides and outfitters.

The mistaken assumption of category homogeneity enters into policy inferences from other quarters as well. In the comprehensive Georgia State *Economic Survey of Wildlife Recreation* (U.S. Forest Service, 1974) a chapter is devoted to how hunters and fishermen rate the "quality aspects" of their sport. This survey may be subject to criticism in that it makes inferences from group data about what individual sportsmen (or subgroups of sportsmen—which are not recognized) want in the outdoor experience. The assumption is that averages or what the majority of sportsmen desire constitute sufficient information for implementing policy. In reference to fishing it is concluded:

> . . . Among national forest users, there is no pattern to be found indicating a relationship between intensity of use and qualitative opinions. An abundance of fish and the convenience of travel to the fishing site are close rivals for the most important characteristic of quality fishing resources. Either of these factors is clearly more important than a low density for fishermen . . . The presence of trophy fish ranks a distant last in importance as a quality fishing resource. (65)

Rule of the averages or majority continues in regard to conclusions on hunting preferences:

> An abundance of game and the convenience of travel to the hunting area rank as the most important qualitative factors affecting the hunting experience in the judgment of southeastern hunting households. . . . while the presence of trophy animals ranks a distant last. (67)

Such reliance on *group* data fails to take into account the preferences of *individual* sportsmen. In other words, variations in the data which comprise the averages are ignored.

2. The fact that the specialization principle is based on reinforcement theory means that there is already a "proven technology" with which managers can respond and shape the demands and behavior of recreationists. Behavior modification principles do work in the outdoor environment (e.g., Clark, et al., 1972). It is a matter of determining what constitutes reward for different groups of rec-

reationists and assessing supply and demand for particular resources. The task is then to apply an information and incentive system to match the user with the most appropriate resource available, managed to meet his needs.

3. One of the most important implications of this research has to do with the satisfactions sportsmen will receive if management decisions are guided by specialization principles. Having made the case that the "quality" outdoor experience depends on what the individual sportsman is looking for and how much of it he gets, ready identification of various sportsmen constituencies will enable the resource manager to maximize satisfaction. In short, he will have a tool with which to identify the sportsman and then match him with the type of setting he requires. Further, it will be managed in so far as possible to further maximize the satisfaction with the experience.

As an example, one of the most frequent complaints from people who camp in state parks and other developed campgrounds has to do with late night noise. Identification of the different types of campers who use these areas might reveal that most of the conflict is between those who visit the campground for sociability reasons and those with more specialized interests. In the case of the former, the desired experience is perhaps to sit around a campfire, talk with friends, and listen to music late into the night. In the case of the latter, the nature and natural attributes of the setting may be the sought after experience. Or they may be anglers who desire to get up early for the best fishing. At present, the only type of management delineation likely to be seen is between tent campers and those with recreational vehicles. Yet it would be a simple matter to segregate campers on the basis of response to a three or four item questionnaire filled out as the camper registers.

4. Not to be overlooked are the political implications of a management policy based on a clear and well established principle of optimum benefits for a *variety* of constituencies. The perplexing problem of satisfying the desires of competing users is lessened when there is a clearly stated, rational basis for resource allocation. Competition for scarce resources will not be eliminated, of course. But

a principle of allocation can be established that both the public and policy makers can understand and with which they can abide.

As an example, nowhere is there more evident the need for a sound and clear resource allocation and management rationale than in the highly controversial issue of "put-and-take" versus "wild trout" fishery policies. And nowhere is there more evident the need of integrating decisions based on "good biology" with those based on "good sociology." Biologists are making a convincing case that a move should be made, where possible, away from stocking toward wild-stream maintenance. The fact that such a policy may require low or no-kill limits and a ban on worm or spinfishing in certain stream sections helps explain the current polarization between fly-fishermen and anglers who use bait, hardware, and other methods to take trout. One writer reports:

> In an effort to maintain wild trout, or just keep the fish big, some states maintain flyfishing-only stretches, with no-catch or one-catch limits, or maybe a limit of one fish over 20 inches long. Pennsylvania has 30 such stretches. One resident, obviously not a flyfisherman, filed a class-action suit against the fish commission for discriminating against his right to fish the way he wanted, where he wanted. (Miller, 1977:128)

The writer goes on to conclude that management decisions

> . . . should ultimately rest on biologists' findings, and should be made in the best interests of the continuing health of the fish populations—not the creel limits or political considerations (128)

The point to be made here is that the conclusions of biologists cannot be effectively implemented without the intersection of their findings with those of social and behavioral scientists. The current findings with regard to recreational specialization not only have obvious and ready applicability for reducing the within-sport conflict described above, but the management scheme they imply provides a logic that most sportsmen would be willing to accept out of a sense of fairness.

SPECIALIZATION AND FUTURE RESEARCH

The specialization principle suggests a number of areas in which social and behavioral research on outdoor recreation is needed:

1. *Additional research to develop classification of sportsmen by user types.* The effort would be a continuation of the research presented in this report. Empirical data would be collected on a variety of outdoor recreationists to further identify and refine the applicability of the specialization principle. A major focus would be the determination of the differing objectives of various recreationists.

2. *Research to trace the developmental aspects of outdoor recreation activity.* How are sportsmen "careers" begun? Do (and how do) orientations and preferences change in the course of time? How are these manifested in behavior? Such inquiry would provide a basis for understanding the dynamics of outdoor recreation behavior and make possible projection of future trends.

3. *Research into the factors which enhance or detract from satisfaction by different sportsmen constituencies.* Much is heard about the "quality" of an outdoor recreation experience (or lack of it). Though the term means different things to different people, operationally it denotes the relationship between what people seek in the outdoors and how much of what they seek they get. Specific factors need to be identified which intervene in the satisfaction of sportsmen desires. Included in this research would be an inventory of conflicts (as well as complementarities) among users of outdoor recreation resources. This would amount to a problem analysis of competitive or conflicting usage by different interests.

4. *Research into the resource preferences of different users.* Since this and other research reveals that ". . . different recreation resources have different attributes of diverse importance of users" (Talhelm, 1973:21), future investigations should be focused on the delineation of *which* resources have *what* importance to *which* users.

5. *Research to assess the impact of recreation management based on the specialization principle.* The utility and desirability of a management strategy which recognizes different recreationist constituencies needs to be established by carefully controlled studies. Though the face validity of such a strategy is strong, an experiment-

al study is needed comparing satisfaction of recreationists and benefits to managers of traditional approaches to those of an approach
based on the specialization principle.

REFERENCES

Clark, Roger N., Robert L. Burgess, and John C. Hendee
    1972 "The development of anti-litter behavior in a Forest Campground."
        Journal of Applied Behavior Analysis 5:1-5.
Miller, Peter
    1977 "The great put-and-take controversy." Outdoor Life 159 (April) :61-128.
Talhelm, Daniel R.
    1973 "Defining and evaluating recreation quality." Pp. 20-28 in John C. Hen-
        dee and Clay Schoenfeld (eds.), Human Dimensions in Wildlife Pro-
        grams: Reports of Recent Investigations. Rockville, Md.: Mercury Press.
USDA Forest Service, Southern Region Number 8
    1974 Economic Survey of Wildlife Recreation. Georgia State University. At-
        lanta: Environmental Research Group.

Printed in the United States
203448BV00003B/232-435/P

9 780817 355197